That Patchwork Place ®

More Template~Free™ Quiltmaking©

by Trudie Hughes, 1987

Acknowledgments

My special thanks to all my Quilt Like Crazy students who trusted me and urged me to find more and more designs for classes. Their enthusiasm has kept me excited about quiltmaking.

All I accomplish is due to the support, love, and encouragement I receive from the crew at Patched Works: Darlene Hays, Judy Konkol, Florence Melster, Nancy Berndt, Gail Salentine, and Pam Quebbeman. They have seen me through some rough times and still found joy and fun in our quiltmaking.

And thanks to Judy Konkol who hand-quilted my Farmer's Stepdaughter wallhanging. Her tireless efforts on my quilts do not go unappreciated.

But most of all, I dedicate this book to Darlene Hays. No amount of thanks could repay her help in reading, rereading, and rereading this manuscript; in recalculating all the quilts; and in running my business so I could make all the quilts.

CREDITS:
Photography ....Carl Murray
Illustration and Graphics..................................Stephanie Benson
Jane Pieplow

All quilts made by author unless otherwise noted.

More Template-Free™ Quiltmaking
©by Trudie Hughes, 1987

Printed in the United States of America
93 92 91   8 7 6 5

ISBN 0-943574-39-0

Library of Congress Card Number: 86-051624

Contents

Introduction

The response to my first book, **Template-Free™ Quiltmaking,** was so overwhelming, that I soon realized I needed to come up with more patterns that use these techniques. It seemed that everyone who experimented with the patterns became eager to do more.

I spend much of my time exploring existing designs and adapting them to the rotary cutter. As a result, I have asked for permission to include other quiltmakers' designs in this book. Judy Martin's Colorado Lob Cabin and Marsha McCloskey's Goose in the Pond have so excited my classes that I wanted to share the techniques of duplicating them in this book.

I am the first to admit that I am not a designer, but rather a "quilt technician." I become consumed with the making of quilts, often making several quilts in a week. It is so much fun, that I never get tired of making them. I have to admit, however, that having a quilt shop with 3,000 bolts of fabric at my disposal doesn't hurt. It makes it hard to avoid becoming a "fabric-aholic." When lots of new fabrics arrive in one day, I go on a "sewing frenzy." I love using different combinations of fabric and seeing designs come to life in a short period of time.

All the quilts in the book were made within three months. Except for the Farmer's Stepdaughter quilt, all were machine quilted.

I hope you enjoy the patterns in this book. They range from very easy to difficult, but all were fun to piece. Just take care in your cutting, and sew with an accurate 1/4" seam. I have tried to help with tips on cutting and piecing, but it will be up to you to make a prize-winning quilt. Good luck and have fun.

Tools and Rules

Equipment

The secret to this system of quiltmaking is the equipment you use. With the right equipment and techniques, quiltmaking can be accurate as well as fast.

The first thing you will need is a rotary cutter. It comes in 2 sizes, but I recommend the larger heavy-duty one. It is much easier to use and gives you better control. When the cutters first came out, they did not have a good cutting surface, and I almost gave up on them. Then Olfa™ came out with its mat, and it made all the difference in the world. The matte finish helps hold the fabric in place, making it easy to cut on. Also, the mat protects the blade and the table you are cutting on. A mat that allows you to cut the fabric as it comes off the bolt is the best size (approximately 18" x 24").

You will also need a tool, both to measure and to guide your cutter, ensuring a clean, straight cut. The Rotary Rule™ is a cutting tool designed for use in template-free quiltmaking. It is made of 1/4" thick Plexiglas™. Anything thinner would not stabilize the cutter and would most likely get cut up. The Rotary Rule™ has a ruler down its length and is graduated in 1/4" increments across its width so that you can measure right to left. To do more advanced procedures, it is very handy to have 45° angle markings and even nicer to have 60° angles printed on it. The Rotary Rule™ has 3 perpendicular intersecting lines across its width to help you subcut strips with straight square cuts. Dotted lines appear on some of the 1/8" lines. These lines make short work of cutting accurate triangles. You can buy other Plexiglas™ rulers, but make sure they have these features.

In addition to the Rotary Rule, I have developed a smaller ruler, which has many functions. First of all, it extends the 3-1/2" of the Rotary Rule to 7" for wider cuts. It also has markings for additional fast triangles, but best of all, it has Speedys along one edge to make Snowball blocks and similar shapes with ease. My students have found that the 12" length is easy to handle, and that once the fabric has been straightened, strips are easier to cut with the smaller ruler.

In addition to these tools, I find a right triangle very helpful. One that is 12" on a side is the most useful. I like my fluorescent colored one, because when my sewing room looks like a rummage sale, I can find it among the unsorted piles.

It is so important to work with the best tools possible. "The right tool for the right job" is true. Shortcutting some of the boring procedures in quilting gets you to the enjoyable parts faster.

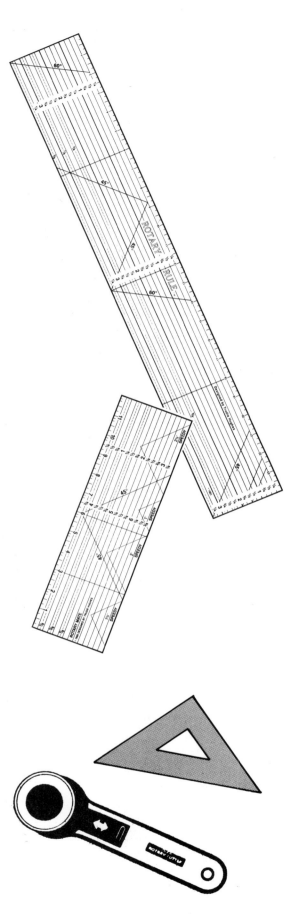

Slice and Dice

It is important to learn to use a rotary cutter accurately and efficiently. Since we want to work with straight pieces, we must learn to cut perfectly straight strips.

The first step is to straighten the fabric. Threads in fabric are often far from perpendicular these days, making it almost impossible to truly straighten fabric, so we will be working with "close grain." You will need to make clean cuts, rather than cuts that are exactly on the straight of grain.

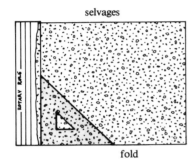

1. Fold fabric in half, selvage to selvage, the way it comes off the bolt.

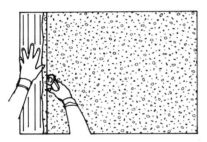

2. Lay triangle along folded edge of fabric and push against right side of ruler until you are just at edge. (If you are right-handed, the bulk of the fabric should be coming from the right.)

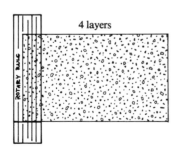

3. Hold ruler down with your left hand and begin cutting slightly in front of fold. Walk your hand up parallel with cutter and continue to cut off end of fabric. If you try to hold onto ruler at the bottom and cut to the end of it, you most likely will move it and therefore cut inaccurately. This is the only time you will have to cut such a long slice.

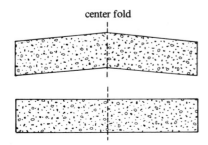

4. Then, fold the fabric one more time, lining up cut edges. Using markings on ruler, cut appropriate strip width. Now cuts can be made only 11" long, which is much easier. Check about every 18" along length of fabric to see if you are still straight. Open up fabric and use triangle and ruler again to check if you are still perpendicular to first fold.

If cuts are not perpendicular to fold, strips will have V shapes when you open them up. Everything is cut selvage to selvage, so you soon will become aware of this.

When you need to cut fabric wider than 3½", you can combine width of ruler with any portion of the Rotary Mate™. You will find most cuts in this book are 3½" or less. If you have cuts wider than the 2 rulers combined, use side of longer ruler to measure off desired width.

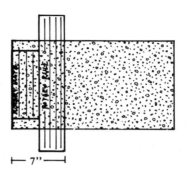

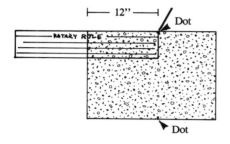

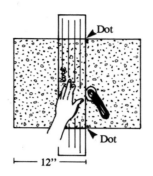

Subcutting into Squares and Rectangles

Some designs will require independent squares or rectangles. These "loose" units will be cut from strips.

Cut strips width of unit plus seam allowances. Then, working with at least 4 layers at a time, straighten left edge of strips (usually has selvages and maybe a fold) by placing cut edge on halfway line of ruler and making a perpendicular slice.

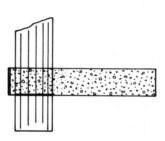

Then, measure left to right, cutting squares same width as strips.

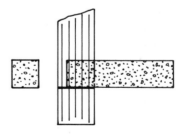

Rectangles are measured by using long side of ruler.

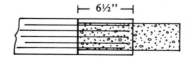

Subcutting Sewn Strips

Many designs begin merely as cut strips. These strips are sewn together, pressed, and then cut again. Four patches and nine patches are best pieced this way and these units occur over and over in other pieced blocks.

In a four patch, sew together 2 sets of contrasting strips.

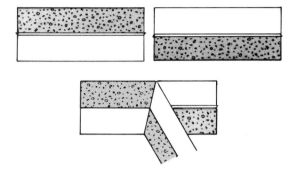

Press consistently toward the same color.

Then, place these 2 sets of sewn strips right sides together. Because of your pressing, you will find seam allowances already going in opposite directions.

Trim the selvages off and cut in pairs from left to right. When you sew these pairs together, there is no need to match or layer; they are ready to feed through the sewing machine in chain fashion.

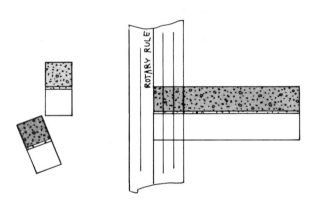

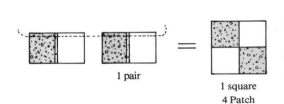

In a nine patch, the same technique is used. However, now you have 3 sets of 3 sewn strips.

Place rows 1 and 2 together. Cut into pairs and sew together in chain fashion.

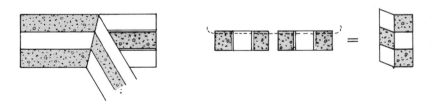

Row 3 is cut by itself.

These three rows are then sewn together.

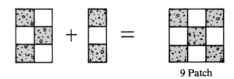

Sewing Guidelines

The other invaluable quilting tool is the sewing machine. The sewing machine has been given a bad name in quiltmaking, yet it has been used in making quilts for the past 125 years. There are machine-made quilts dated the same year as its introduction.

Along with cutting accurately, sewing accurately will yield pieced quilt tops of which you can be proud. No one enjoys sewing and resewing to make things come out correctly. Here are a few guidelines to help you keep on track. Usually, when I see work that looks sloppy or haphazardly pieced, one of these rules was broken.

SINCE 1/4" SEAM ALLOWANCES ARE ADDED TO ALL CUT PIECES, YOU MUST LEARN TO SEW 1/4" SEAMS. Very few machines have a presser foot exactly 1/4" wide. If you are lucky enough to have one, be happy, as most of us do not.

Normally, you will have to establish where to look ON THE PRESSER FOOT as a guide to yield the correct seam, because you often will not be able to see the bed of the machine. Therefore, any markings on the bed, such as masking tape or the machine's own markings, will not help you. That method works only if you are sewing independent pieces. To find your guide for a ¼" seam, take a piece of fabric and feed it through your machine at what you feel is ¼" away from the needle. Then, MEASURE IT.

I have a foreign-made machine and the ¼" seam means I must keep the edge of the fabric just under the presser foot. After you practice enough, it becomes easy. People who do a great deal of piecing become so familiar with what a ¼" seam looks like that they can spot anything that deviates from it. When sewing long strips, it is natural to drift, but if you try to remember the trouble it causes, you will stay steady.

WHEN SEWING 2 PIECES TOGETHER THAT SHOULD MATCH, MAKE SURE THEY BEGIN AND END MATCHED. All machines have a tendency to shift layers of fabric. If you think of your machine as an opponent that is purposely trying to shift everything, then hold on and make sure it can't. I do not pin, but if you feel it will ensure that the pieces match, by all means pin.

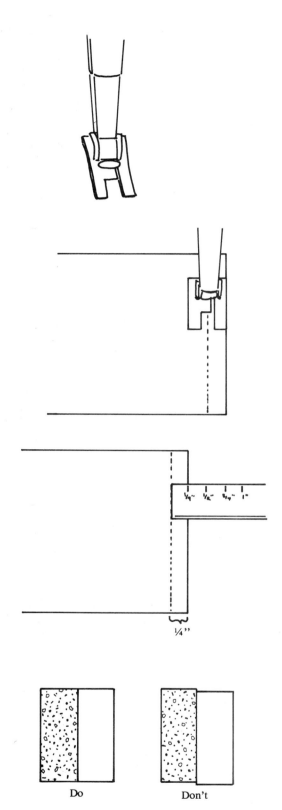

¼"

Do   Don't

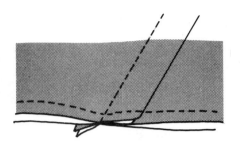

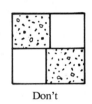

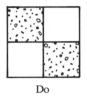

Do   Don't

WHEN COMING TO INTERSECTING SEAMS, SEAM ALLOWANCES SHOULD ALWAYS LIE IN OPPOSITE DIRECTIONS. Your machine wants to jog any bulky areas. If you line up all seams on the same side, it will most likely move one. By having seams in opposite directions, the bulk is reduced and seams hug the intersection. You want this intersection to look crisp from the front. It is not unusual in machine piecing to have seams twist and change directions, in order to make seam allowances go in opposite directions.

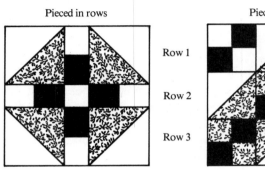

Pieced in rows   Pieced in rows

Row 1   Row 1
Row 2   Row 2
Row 3   Row 3

In most machine-pieced designs, blocks are pieced in rows or in quarters. If you take a minute to decide which way would be best for the particular block you are working on, you can be more efficient in your piecing.

Pieced in quarters   Pieced in rows   Pieced in quarters

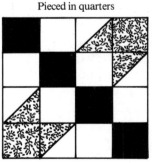
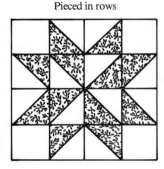
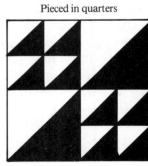

As a rule, seams are not pressed open in machine piecing. They are pressed to one side, usually toward the darker fabric. When pressing sets of strips, press from the right side. That way they are pressed completely flat, and you are less likely to press pleats at the seams. On many patterns, the direction of the pressing is the key to ensuring a neat and correctly pieced quilt.

Quilt Patterns

For each quilt you will find a piecing diagram labeled with the number of blocks and the dimensions before and after the various borders. You can use this information to vary the size of the quilts you make.

Fabric requirements are given to duplicate the quilts photographed for the book. Fabric used for the borders and binding is given separately so you may make changes. The pieced borders are another option you may use to vary your quilt.

The directions on the following pages are written "recipe-style" for your convenience. Cutting requirements are grouped according to the fabric being cut. You will save time by handling each fabric only once, cutting all the necessary strips and pieces. The fabric to be cut is printed in bold face type followed by the cutting directions for the quilt and optional pieced border. Ignore the pieced border cutting directions if you are not using a pieced border on your quilt. I rounded all the yardages up a bit to accommodate at least one more strip than needed (in case you goof). If you are nervous about not having enough fabric, I suggest adding 1/8 yd. to your purchase.

Each pattern includes tips on cutting the shapes involved. Where appropriate, I also have added tips on piecing. There always seem to be tricks in putting each quilt together. All of the quilts in the book have been made more than once. I tried to make the quilt at the same time I wrote the directions, so I could pass on any easier methods I discovered.

How you finish these tops is up to you. At the end of the book, I have included my methods of layering, binding and machine quilting. If you are a hand-quilter, you will like the patterns, because they will get you to quilting faster. Have fun!

Quilts Made with Strips

Strip Rail

This quilt may look familiar. It is a different version of the Strip Bow quilt from my first book. I have included it here, because it is so simple to make. When the blocks are pieced and arranged in this manner, it looks like an interesting rail fence design.

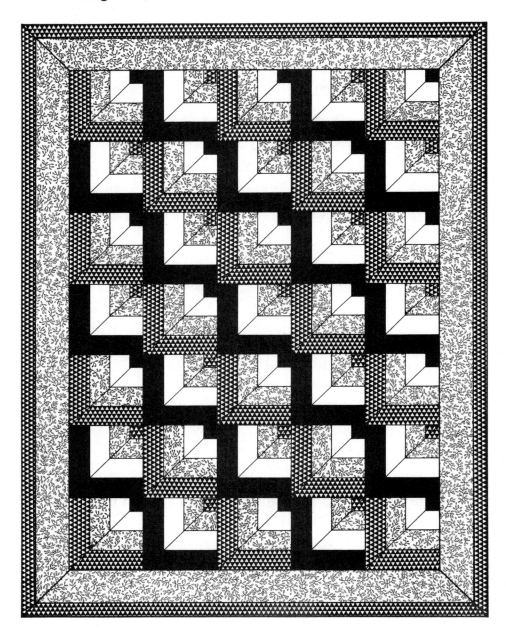

Crib Quilt (Pictured on page 41)

35 pieced blocks, set 5 blocks by 7 blocks.
Piecing area finishes to 27-1/2'' by 38-1/2''.
After border, quilt will be 33-1/2'' by 44-1/2''.

Fabric Requirements

Pieced area—1/2 yd. each of 4 fabrics
Border fabric—5/8 yd.
Binding—1/2 yd.
Backing—1-1/2 yd.

Cutting Requirements

1. Cut 6 strips 2" wide from each of the 4 fabrics for pieced area.
2. Cut 5 strips 3-1/2" wide for border.
3. Cut 5 strips 2-1/2" wide for binding.

Piecing and Assembly

1. First sew the 4 colors of strips together and make a unit. Both blocks are created from the same unit of strips. Each unit will yield 6 blocks. Press all seams in one sewn unit in one direction. Half the units are pressed in one direction and other half will be pressed in opposite direction.

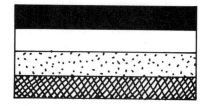

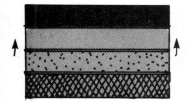 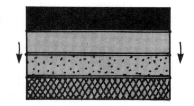

Now, take 2 sets of strips that are pressed in opposite directions and place them with right sides together, matching colors. You will find that seam allowances are now going in opposite directions, reducing the need to line them up when sewn. Measure width of sewn unit and use that measurement to cut strip into squares (they should measure 6-1/2"). Cut these squares with one diagonal cut. The resulting triangles are lined up, ready to sew. Sew down long side and press. You will find 2 types of blocks, which we will alternate in the design.

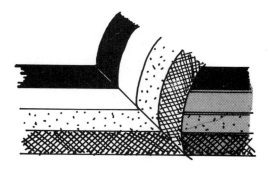

 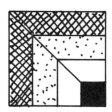

 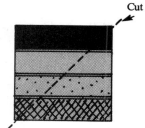

2. Join the blocks into rows according to diagram. Join rows.
3. Add borders.

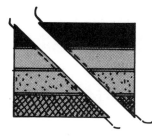

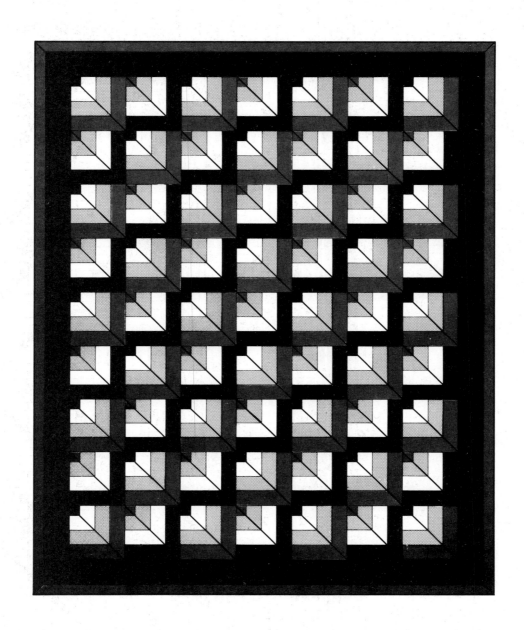

Lap Quilt (pictured on page 41)

63 pieced blocks, set 7 blocks by 9 blocks.
Piecing area finishes to 38-1/2'' by 49-1/2''.
After border, quilt will be 44-1/2'' by 55-1/2''.

Fabric Requirements

Pieced area—1 yd. each of 4 fabrics
Border fabric—1 yd.
Binding—3/4 yd.
Backing—3 yds. (pieced crosswise)

Cutting Requirements

1. Cut 11 strips 2'' wide from each of the 4 fabrics for pieced area.
2. Cut 6 strips 3-1/2'' wide for border.
3. Cut 6 strips 2-1/2'' wide for binding.

Piecing and Assembly

Follow instructions given for crib quilt on page 13. You will need to piece 63 blocks and sew them together, 7 blocks across by 9 blocks down.

Chimneys and Cornerstones

Large Quilt (pictured on page 42)

Chimneys and Cornerstones

This traditional pattern is ageless. It can lend itself to either a contemporary or an old country setting. The rotary cutter makes it easy to cut and piece.

It is easy to select fabric for this quilt. You need to choose one fabric for the light sides; the dark sides contain 4 dark fabrics. You also need to select the accent fabric for the contrasting squares, which form the diagonal lines in the log cabin blocks.

Large Quilt (pictured on page 42)

80 pieced blocks, set 8 blocks by 10 blocks.
Piecing area finishes to 72" by 90".
After first border, quilt will be 75" by 93".
After pieced border, quilt will be 81" by 99".
After last border, quilt will be 87" by 105".

Fabric Requirements

Light—4-1/4 yds. (3-1/2 yds. for piecing, 3/4 yd. for pieced border)
Accent—3-1/2 yds. (1-1/4 yds. for piecing, 1/2 yd. for pieced border, 3/4 yd. for first border, 1 yd. for binding)
First dark—1/2 yd.
Second dark—7/8 yd.
Third dark—1-3/4 yds. (1-1/4 yds. for piecing, 1/2 yd. for pieced border)
Darkest—3-3/4 yds. (1-1/2 yds. for piecing, 1 yd. for pieced border, and 1-1/4 yds. for last border)
Backing—9-1/2 yds. (You can get one or more borders from excess width.)

Cutting Requirements

Light

Cut 3 strips each, of the following widths: 1-1/2", 2-1/2", 3-1/2", 4-1/2", 5-1/2", 6-1/2", 7-1/2", and 8-1/2". Subcut all these strips, except 1-1/2" width, into 1-1/2" segments. You should get 28 cuts from each strip.

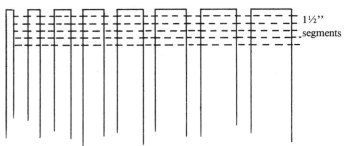

1½" segments

For pieced border:

1. Cut 2 strips 4-1/4" wide into 15 squares. Then cut these with an X to yield the 58 quarter-square triangles needed.

2. Cut 6 strips 1-1/2" wide into 62 decapitated triangles, measuring along cut edge at 4-1/4" intervals. (See page 60 for details on cutting these.)

Accent

1. Cut 27 strips 1-1/2" wide.
2. Cut 10 strips 2" wide for first border.
3. Cut 11 strips 2-1/2" wide for binding.

For pieced border:

1. Cut 2 strips 4-1/4" wide into 15 squares. Then, cut these with an X to yield the 58 quarter-square triangles needed.

2. Cut 5 strips 1-1/2" wide into 54 decapitated triangles, measuring along cut edge at 4-1/4" intervals.

3. Cut 4 squares 1-1/2" for corner units.

First dark

Cut 3 strips 1-1/2" wide and 3 strips 2-1/2" wide.

Second dark

Cut 3 strips 3-1/2" wide and 3 strips 4-1/2" wide.

Third dark

Cut 3 strips 5-1/2" wide and 3 strips 6-1/2" wide.

For pieced border:

Cut 6 strips 1-7/8'' wide into 112 squares. Then, cut these diagonally into 224 triangles.

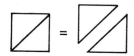

Darkest

1. Cut 3 strips 7-1/2'' wide and 3 strips 8-1/2'' wide.
2. Cut 11 strips 3-1/2'' wide for last border.

For pieced border:

1. Cut 4 strips 4-1/4'' wide into 29 squares. Then cut these with an X to yield the 116 quarter-square triangles needed.

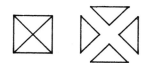

2. Cut 5 strips 1-1/2'' into 54 rectangles 1-1/2'' by 3-1/2''.

3. Cut 1 strip 1-1/2'' wide into 8 trapezoids, measuring along cut edge at 2-7/8'' intervals. (See page 67 for more details on cutting these.)

Piecing and Assembly

One 9'' block looks like this:

1. Sew an accent strip to each dark fabric strip and to each 1-1/2'' wide light strip. Press seams toward accent fabric and subcut into 1-1/2'' segments. These can be stacked to speed up the cutting.

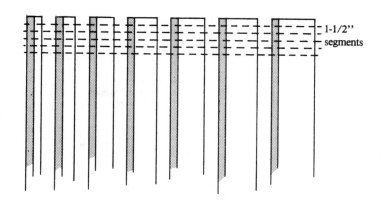

2. Working in a circle, alternately sew light strips and dark strips (with their accent squares attached). Press seams of light strips toward center. Press seams of dark strips toward outside. This will help match seams of accent squares.

3. Sew blocks together in a barnraising setting.
4. Sew on the first border, measuring proper lengths and matching centers and ends of border strips with quilt.

CREATIVE OPTION

After sewing on the first border, you may add this pieced border. It has 2 basic units and corners. Each finishes to 3''. Since you are alternating 2 blocks, you need odd numbers of units to make up a side.

From each 4-1/4'' wide strip, you will get 36 quarter-square triangles.
From each 1-7/8'' wide strip, you will get 44 triangles.
From each 1-1/2'' wide strip, you will get 12 decapitated triangles.
From each 1-1/2'' wide strip, you will get 12 cuts 3-1/2'' long for rectangles.

1. Make 58 A blocks that look like this:

Piece 58 quarter-square triangles of medium fabric to 58 light quarter-square triangles, and 58 quarter-square triangles of medium fabric to 58 accent quarter-square triangles.

2. Make 54 B blocks that look like this:

Sew triangles to each side of all light and accent decapitated triangles. Sew these alternately with rectangles.

3. Make 4 corner units that look like this:

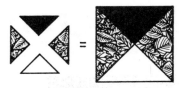

Sew trapezoids to small square. Then, add a triangle to one side of each decapitated triangle; add these to complete corner. See Attic Window piecing and assembly on page 71.

4. Alternating A units and B units, sew 2 border strips of 31 units each. Begin and end each strip with an A unit. Sew these strips to long sides of quilt.

5. Alternating A units and B units, sew 2 border strips of 25 units each. Begin and end each strip with an A unit. Sew a corner unit onto each end and add to quilt at top and bottom.

6. Add last border.

Lap Quilt (pictured on page 44)

24 pieced blocks, set 4 blocks by 6 blocks
Piecing area finishes to 36'' by 54''.
After first border, quilt will be 39'' by 57''.
After pieced border, quilt will be 45'' by 63''.
After last border, quilt will be 49'' by 67''.

Fabric Requirements

Light—1-3/4 yds. (1-1/4 yds. for piecing, 1/2 yd. for pieced border)
Accent—2 yds. (1/2 yd. for piecing, 1/2 yd. for pieced border. 1 yd. for first and last border)
First Dark—5/8 yd. (1/4 yd. for piecing, 3/8 yd. for pieced border)
Second Dark—1/2 yd.
Third Dark—1/2 yd.
Fourth Dark—1-3/4 yds.(3/4 yd. for piecing, 1/4 yd. for pieced border, 3/4 yd. for binding)
Darkest—1/2 yd. for pieced border
Backing—4 yds.

Cutting Requirements

Light

Cut 1 strip each, of the following widths: 1-1/2", 2-1/2", 3-1/2", 4-1/2", 5-1/2", 6-1/2", 7-1/2", and 8-1/2". Subcut all these strips, except 1-1/2" width, into 1-1/2" segments.

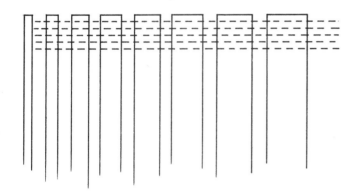

For pieced border:

1.   Cut 1 strip 4-1/4" wide into 9 squares, then cut these squares with an X to yield the 34 quarter-square triangles needed.

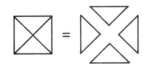

2.   Cut 3 strips 1-1/2" wide into 30 decapitated triangles, measuring along cut edge at 4-1/4" intervals. (See page 60 for more details on cutting these.)

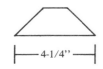

3.   Cut 4 squares 1-1/2" for corners.

Accent

1.   Cut 9 strips 1-1/2" wide.
2.   Cut 5 strips 2" wide for first border.
3.   Cut 7 strips 2-1/2" wide for last border.

For pieced border:

Cut 3 strips 1-7/8" wide into 64 squares, then cut these diagonally to yield 128 loose triangles.

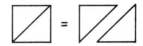

First Dark

Cut 1 strip 1-1/2" wide and 1 strip 2-1/2" wide.

For pieced border:

Cut 2 strips 4-1/4" wide into 17 squares, then cut these with an X to yield the 68 quarter-square triangles needed.

Second Dark

Cut 1 strip 3-1/2" wide and 1 strip 4-1/2" wide.

Third Dark

Cut 1 strip 5-1/2" wide and 1 strip 6-1/2" wide.

Fourth Dark

1.   Cut 1 strip 7-1/2" wide and 1 strip 8-1/2" wide.
2.   Cut 7 strips 2-1/2" wide for binding.

For pieced border:

1.   Cut 3 strips 1-1/2" wide into 30 rectangles, each 1-1/2" by 3-1/2".
2.   Cut 1 strip 1-1/2" wide into 8 trapezoids for corners, measuring along cut edge at 2-7/8" intervals. (See page 67 for more details on cutting these.)

20

Darkest

For pieced border:

    1.   Cut 4 strips 1-1/2" wide for 38 decapitated triangles, measuring along cut edge at 4-1/4" intervals.

    2.   Cut 1 strip 4-1/4" wide into 9 squares. Then, cut these with an X to yield the 34 quarter-square triangles needed.

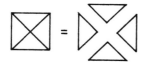

Piecing and Assembly

    1.   Follow instructions given for large quilt on page 17. You will need to piece 24 blocks and sew them together in a barnraising setting, 4 blocks by 6 blocks.

    2.   Sew on first border, measuring proper lengths and matching centers and ends of border strips with quilt.

CREATIVE OPTION

    After adding the first border, a pieced border can be added to this quilt. Refer to instructions given for large quilt.

    1.   Alternating A units and B units, make 2 border strips of 19 units each. Begin and end with an A unit. Sew these strips to sides of quilt.

    2.   Alternating A units and B units, make 2 border strips of 13 units each. Begin and end with an A unit. Add a corner unit to each end of these border strips. Add to quilt at top and bottom.

    3.   Add last border.

Quilts Made with Squares and Triangles

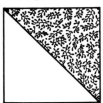

Half-Square Triangles

You will need squares and triangles to make the quilts in this section of the book. For some quilts the triangles are cut individually, then sewn to other shapes. I refer to these as loose half-square triangles.

In many of the quilts, two triangles are sewn together to form a square. When this shape appears often in a quilt, use fast sewn half-square triangles.

Loose Half-Square Triangles

Cut a strip the desired finished measurement plus 7/8".

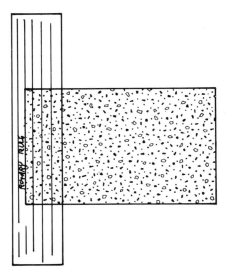

Then subcut into squares with the same measurement.

4 layers

Take a stack of 4 squares and cut diagonally corner to corner. These triangles are now the right size to mix with the other shapes.

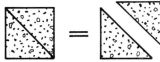

Fast Sewn Half-Square Triangles

Fast triangles are not new. Many have written about them; you can hardly pick up a pattern anymore without running into instructions that use this technique. However, some of these instructions tell you to add 1'' to the measurement of the triangle. Adding 1'' is a 1/8'' miscalculation. Multiplied over many pieces, this can add up to a big headache. Things suddenly don't fit, and it can be very discouraging.

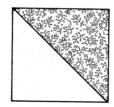

Half-Square Triangles

When you are making patterns where 2 different color triangles are sewn together to form a square, you should sew them first.

Establish 2 perpendicular lines with your triangle. Draw these lines on the lightest fabric.

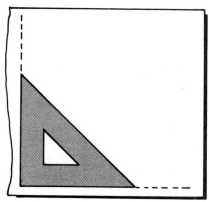

Light fabric on top, dark fabric underneath, right sides together.

Working with 2 fat quarters of fabric (each 18'' by 22'') placed right sides together, mark a grid of squares with the formula: the finished size of the triangle plus 7/8''. For every square you draw, you will get 2 sewn triangle units.

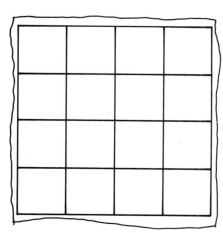

Draw the diagonals through all squares, first in one direction, marking every other row of squares. Then mark the alternate squares with a diagonal in the opposite direction.

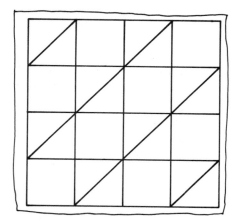
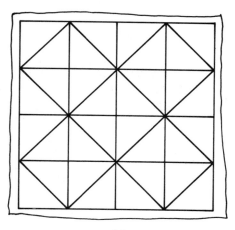

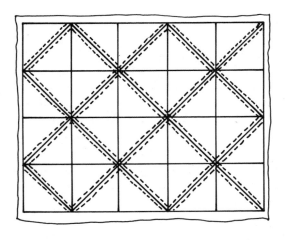

If you have established where 1/4'' is on your presser foot, you can use that as a guide and stitch a 1/4'' seam on both sides of all diagonals. Because of the way you have drawn the diagonals, you can keep stitching without stopping. It reminds me of when I learned to draw a house with one continuous line in the third grade. This triangle method is still as exciting to me now as drawing the house was then.

If you have trouble with the proper seam allowance, use your ruler to mark 1/4'' lines on each side of the diagonals and stitch on the lines. It will be slower but more accurate.

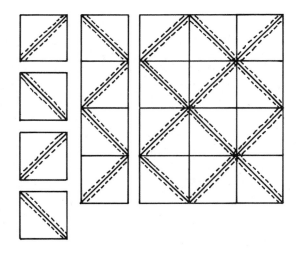

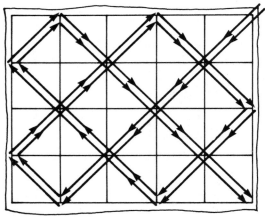

After these are sewn, cut them apart exactly on the drawn lines. I found that if you cut them into squares first, you can clip out the points before you subcut them into triangles. Then these points are not in the way when pressing or sewing into the design. When these 2 triangles are sewn next to each other, the resulting square will measure correctly.

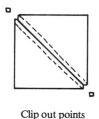

Clip out points

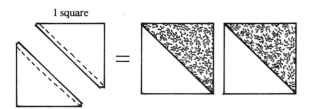

1 square

Scrap-aholic

If you are not a fabric-aholic before you begin this quilt, you will become one soon after. It is so much fun to piece, that rarely does anyone make just one.

The scrap quilt looks more difficult to piece than it is. First, you will need to sort your scraps into light and dark fabrics. I try to eliminate plaids, stripes, and patchwork printed fabrics. Unless I will be using lots of solid fabrics, I do not use any solids either. The quilt looks best if there is a definite distinction between light and dark. You probably will not have enough light fabrics. Over the years, my students have had this similar problem: lots of dark colors but very few light background fabrics. If you don't have enough, you may want to start collecting quarter yards of light fabrics as you find them in your favorite fabric haunts.

In the smaller quilt, I used a black solid fabric for the center square. In the larger quilt, I used various scraps for this square.

Lap Quilt (not pictured)

48 pieced blocks, set 6 blocks by 8 blocks
Piecing area finishes to 45" by 60".
After borders, quilt will be 51" by 66".

Large Quilt (pictured on page 43)

Large Quilt (pictured on page 43)

120 blocks, set 10 blocks by 12 blocks
Piecing area finishes to 75" by 90".
After first border, quilt will be 80" by 95".
After pieced border, quilt will be 85" by 100".
After last border, quilt will be 90" by 105".

Fabric Requirements

Light—1 yd. of assorted prints for crib size (start
    with at least 12 different ones)
    2 yds. of assorted prints for lap size
    4 yds. of assorted prints for large size

Dark—1 yd. of assorted prints for crib size (start
    with at least 12 different ones)
    2 yds. of assorted prints for lap size
    4 yds. of assorted prints for large size

Accent—5/8 yd. for crib size (1/4 yd. for center
    squares, 3/8 yd. for first border)

Border—3/4 yd. for crib size (second border)
    1 yd. for lap size
    2 yds. for large size

Binding—1/2 yd. for crib size
    3/4 yd. for lap size
    1 yd. for large size

Backing—1-3/4 yds. for crib size
    4 yds. for lap size
    9-1/2 yds. for large size

Cutting Requirements

Light

1. Cut fabrics into 3" squares. You will need 3 light squares per block.
2. Set aside some pieces to be used for fast triangles. You will need 2 fast triangles per block.

Dark

1. Cut fabrics into 3" squares. You will need 4 dark squares per block (only 3 per block if you use a solid for the center square).
2. Set aside some pieces to be used for fast triangles.

Accent (for crib quilt)

1. Cut 2 strips 3" wide into 24 squares. These will be used as center squares of blocks.
2. Cut 5 strips 2" wide for first border.

Borders

1. Cut 5 strips 3-1/2" wide for crib size (second border).
2. Cut 7 strips 3-1/2" wide for lap size.
3. Cut 18 strips 3" wide for large size.

Binding

1. Cut 5 strips 2-1/2" wide for crib size.
2. Cut 7 strips 2-1/2" wide for lap size.
3. Cut 10 strips 2-1/2" wide for large size.

Piecing and Assembly

1. To make the fast triangles, mark a 3-3/8" grid on light fabric and place right sides together with dark fabric. (See page 23 for detailed directions.)

Note: If you have a large piece of light fabric, you can mark the grid but cut out different numbers of squares to sew to different darks.

2. Piece 7-1/2" blocks to look like this:

Row 1
Row 2
Row 3

3. To use a barnraising setting, sew blocks in rows with an even number of blocks across and an even number of blocks down.

The crib quilt takes 24 blocks, set 4 blocks by 6 blocks.

The lap quilt takes 48 blocks, set 6 blocks by 8 blocks.

The large quilt takes 120 blocks, set 10 blocks by 12 blocks.

4. Add borders.

CREATIVE OPTION

After sewing on the first border, you may add a pieced border to the large quilt.

1. Cut 144 squares, each 3", from assorted dark fabrics.
2. Piece 32 squares into a strip. Add to top edge. Repeat for bottom.
3. Add a strip of 40 squares to each side.
4. Add last border.

Crib Quilt (pictured on page 44)

24 pieced blocks, set 4 blocks by 6 blocks
Piecing area finishes to 30" by 45".
After borders, quilt will be 39" by 54".

Road to Oklahoma

Lap Quilt (pictured on page 45)

24 pieced blocks, set 4 blocks by 6 blocks with 2"
 lattice strips
Piecing area finishes to 42" by 62".
After last border, quilt will be 48" by 68".

Road to Oklahoma

This quilt is made up of simple ingredients: four-patches, loose squares, and fast triangles. The secret to its beauty is the way the fabrics are used. There is just one 8" pieced block, yet it is colored 3 different ways.

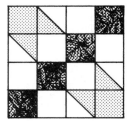

Light background

Medium background

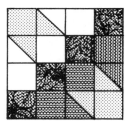

Half light and half medium background

Begin by selecting 2 different background fabrics, one very light and the other a medium-toned fabric. Next, select a dark fabric for the small squares that run through the quilt. Then, select a contrast fabric to make up the stars.

Fabric Requirements

Light background—1 yd.
Medium background—2 yds. (3/4 yds. for piecing,
    1-1/4 yds. for lattice)
Dark—1-1/2 yds. (3/4 yds. for piecing, 3/4 yd. for
    border)
Accent—2 yds. (1-1/4 yds. for piecing, 3/4 yd. for
    binding)
Backing—3 yds. (pieced crosswise)

Cutting Requirements

Light background

1. Cut 4 strips 2-1/2'' wide for four-patches.
2. Cut 2 strips 2-1/2'' wide into 28 squares.
3. Set aside rest of light fabric to mark fast
triangles.

Medium Background

1. Cut 3 strips 2-1/2'' wide for four-patches.
2. Cut 2 strips 2-1/2'' wide into 20 squares.
3. Cut 15 strips 2-1/2'' wide, then cut these into
58 rectangles 2-1/2'' by 8-1/2'' for lattice.
4. Set aside rest of medium fabric for fast
triangles.

Dark

1. Cut 7 strips 2-1/2'' wide for four-patches.
2. Cut 2 strips 2-1/2'' wide into 18 squares to be
used in lattice.
3. Cut 7 strips 3-1/2'' wide for border.

Accent (Stars)

1. Cut 5 strips 2-1/2'' wide into 65 squares.
2. Cut 7 strips 2-1/2'' wide for binding.
3. Set aside rest of accent fabric for fast
triangles.

Piecing and Assembly

1. On light background fabric, mark a 2-7/8''
grid of squares, 5 by 6, and place right sides
together with accent fabric. Stitch 1/4'' seam on
both sides of drawn diagonal lines. Cut apart and
press. Set aside.

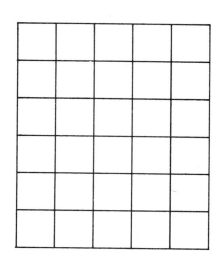

Make 56 triangle units that look like this:

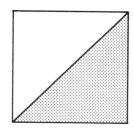

2. On medium fabric, mark a 2-7/8'' grid of
squares, 4 by 5, and place right sides together with
accent fabric. Stitch, cut apart, and press. Set aside.

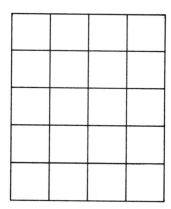

Make 40 triangle units that look like this:

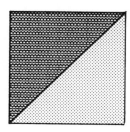

31

3. To make four-patches, sew 4 light fabric strips to 4 dark fabric strips. Sew 3 medium fabric strips to 3 dark fabric strips. (See page 8 for more information on making four-patches.)

Make 16 four-patches of light-dark that look like this:

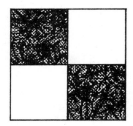

Make 8 four-patches of medium-dark that look like this:

Make 24 mixed four-patches that look like this:

4. Make 8 blocks that look like this:

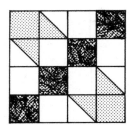

5. Make 4 blocks that look like this:

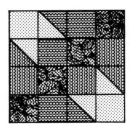

6. Make 12 blocks that look like this:

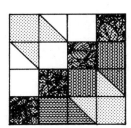

7. Assemble quilt in rows, placing a lattice strip between blocks.

8. Sew lattice strips to accent squares, alternating dark and accent squares with lattice strips.; join rows.

9. Sew on border.

32

Pinwheels in Pinwheels

Large Quilt (not pictured)

24 pieced blocks, set 4 blocks by 6 blocks
Piecing area finishes to 64" by 96".
After first border, quilt will be 72" by 104".
After pieced border, quilt will be 76" by 108"
After last border, quilt will be 80" by 112".

Fabric Requirements

Light—2-1/4 yds. (1-1/2 yds. for piecing, 3/4 yds. for pieced border)
Medium—3-1/2 yds. (2-3/4 yds. for piecing, 3/4 yd. for pieced border)
Dark—5-1/2 yds. (3-3/4 yds. for piecing, 1 yd. for binding, 3/4 yd. for pieced border)
Accent—2-1/4 yds. for first and last borders
Backing—6-3/4 yds.

Cutting Requirements

Light

Mark 96 squares in a 4-7/8" grid, 8 across by 12 down, to yield 192 larger triangle units.

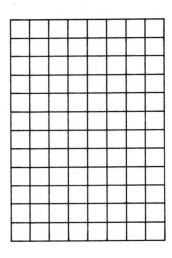 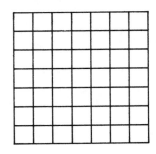

For pieced border:

1. Mark 44 squares in a 2-7/8" grid, 7 across by 7 down, to be sewn with dark fabric.

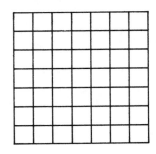

2. Mark 44 squares in a 2-7/8" grid, 7 across by 7 down, to be sewn with medium fabric.

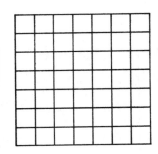

Medium

1. Mark 192 squares with a 2-7/8" grid, 14 across by 14 down, to make the 384 smaller triangles needed. It is easier to sew if you break this unit into 3 sections.

2. Cut 11 strips 4-1/2" wide into 96 squares 4-1/2".

For pieced border:

Set aside a piece of fabric approximately 24" by 24" for fast triangles.

Dark

1. Cut 11 strips 2-1/2" wide for binding.
2. Set aside remainder of fabric. This will be sewn with light and medium fabrics for fast triangles in blocks and pieced border.

Accent

1. Cut 10 strips 4-1/2" wide for first border.
2. Cut 11 strips 2-1/2" wide for last border.

Piecing and Assembly

1. Place light fabric that has been marked with grid on top of dark fabric, right sides together. Do the same with medium fabric that has been marked. Sew a 1/4" seam on each side of diagonal lines. Cut apart; press seams toward dark fabric.

2. First, piece larger blocks in quarters:

3. Then, join quarters to yield 24 blocks.

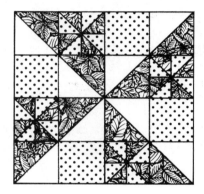

4. Piece these blocks 3 across by 6 down.

5. Add first border, measuring proper lengths and matching centers and ends of border strips with quilt.

CREATIVE OPTION

After sewing on first border, you may add this pieced border. This border alternates 2 flying geese units with 1 unit split for the ends. I find them easier to piece from 2 fast triangles. Since you are already making fast triangles for the pieced area of quilt, you can also make them for the border. When pressing triangles open, press half of seams in one direction, and half in other direction. That way, your seam allowances will be going in opposite directions, and intersections will match.

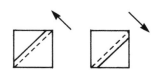

1. Make 44 flying geese A units of medium-light combination that look like this:

2. Make 40 flying geese B units of dark-light combination that look like this:

3. Make 8 triangle units for ends of each border strip that look like this:

4. Mark and sew 2 squares 2-7/8" of the light fabric. Sew to dark fabric to make fast triangles in corner units that look like this:

5. Make top and bottom border strips by sewing 17 flying geese units together. Alternate A units with B units, beginning and ending with an A unit. Add a dark-light triangle unit onto each end. Sew these onto top and bottom of quilt, carefully matching centers and ends.

6. Make side border strips by sewing 25 flying geese units together. Alternate A units with B units, beginning and ending with an A unit. Add dark-light triangle units and medium-dark corner units onto ends. Sew these onto sides of quilt, carefully matching centers and ends.

7. Sew on last border.

Crib Quilt (with first border only)
Lap Quilt (with all borders) (pictured on page 46)

6 pieced blocks, set 2 blocks by 3 blocks
Piecing area finishes to 32" by 48".
After first border, quilt will be 40" by 56".
After pieced border, quilt will be 44" by 60".
After last border, quilt will be 47" by 63".

Fabric Requirements

Light—1-1/2 yds. (1 yd. for piecing, 1/2 yd. for
    pieced border)
Medium—1-3/4 yds. (1-1/4 yds. for piecing, 1/2
    yd. for pieced border)
Dark—2-5/8 yds. (1-1/2 yds. for piecing, 1/2 yd.
    for pieced border, and 5/8 yd. for binding)
Accent—1-1/2 yds. (1 yd. for first border and 1/2
    yd. for last border)
Backing—1-3/4 yds. for crib quilt, 3 yds. for lap
    quilt (pieced crosswise)

Cutting Requirements

Light

Mark 24 squares with a 4-7/8'' grid, 4 across by 6 down. These will be sewn with dark fabric to yield 48 larger triangle units.

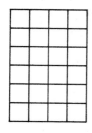 

For pieced border:

1. Mark 24 squares with a 2-7/8'' grid, 4 across by 6 down, to be sewn with medium fabric.

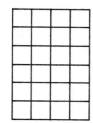

Make 48

2. Mark 24 squares with a 2-7/8'' grid, 4 across by 6 down, to be sewn with dark fabric.

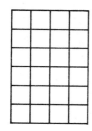

Make 48

Medium

1. Mark 48 squares with a 2-7/8'' grid, 7 across by 7 down, to yield 96 smaller triangle units.

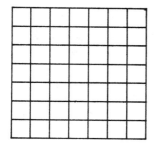

2. Cut 3 strips 4-1/2'' wide into 24 squares.

For pieced border:

1. Set aside a piece of fabric, approximately 14'' by 20'', to be sewn with light fabric for fast triangles.
2. Mark 4 squares with a 2-7/8'' grid. These will be sewn with dark fabric to yield 8 triangle units for corners.

Dark

1. Set aside a piece of fabric, approximately 27'' by 27'' to be sewn with light fabric for larger triangle units.
2. Set aside a piece of fabric, approximately 24'' by 24'', to be sewn with medium fabric for smaller triangle units.
3. Cut 7 strips 2-1/2'' wide for binding (for crib size, cut only 6 strips).

For pieced border:

1. Set aside a piece of fabric, approximately 14'' by 20'', to be sewn with light fabric for fast triangles.
2. Set aside a piece of fabric, approximately 8'' square, to be sewn with medium fabric for fast triangles.

Accent

1. Cut 6 strips 4-1/2'' wide for first border.
2. Cut 7 strips 2'' wide for last border.

Piecing and Assembly

Follow directions given for large quilt, but make only 6 large blocks.

CREATIVE OPTION

After sewing on the first border, you may add this pieced border and an outer border. This will make a lap quilt instead of a crib quilt.

1. Make 24 flying geese A units of medium-light combination that look like this:

2. Make 20 flying geese B units of dark-light combination that look like this:

3. Make 8 triangle units of dark-light for ends of each border strip that look like this:

4. Mark and sew 2 squares 2-7/8" of medium fabric. Sew to dark fabric for fast triangles in corner units that look like this:

5. Sew 9 flying geese units together. Alternate A and B units beginning and ending with an A unit. Add a dark-light triangle unit onto each end. Sew these to top and bottom of quilt, carefully matching centers and ends.

6. Sew 13 flying geese units together. Alternate A and B units, beginning and ending with an A unit. Add dark-light triangle units and medium-dark corner units onto ends. Sew these to sides of quilt, carefully matching centers and ends.

7. Sew on last border.

Goose in the Pond

Large Quilt (pictured on page 47)

39

Goose in the Pond (pictured on page 47)

18 pieced blocks, set diagonally
Piecing area finishes to 60" by 80".
After first border, quilt will be 64" by 84".
After second border, quilt will be 70" by 90".
After pieced border, quilt will be 82" by 102".
After last border, quilt will be 86" by 106".

Fabric Requirements

Light—5-1/4 yds. (2-1/2 yds. for piecing, 2-3/4 yds. for pieced border)
Bright accent—2-3/4 yds. (1-1/2 yds. for piecing, 1/2 yd. for pieced border, 3/4 yds. for first border)
Main dark—6 yds. (3 yds. for piecing, 1 yd. for pieced border, 1 yd. for last border, 1 yd. for binding)
Accent dark—3-1/2 yds. (2-1/2 yds. for piecing, 1 yd. for second border)
Backing—10 yds.

Cutting Requirements

Light

1. Mark 108 squares in a 3-1/8" grid, 10 across by 11 down, to yield 216 triangle units.

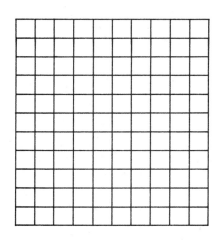

2. Cut 6 strips 2-3/4" wide into 90 squares 2-3/4".
3. Cut 15 strips 1-1/4" wide for nine patches.
4. Cut 6 strips 1-1/4" wide for rails.

For pieced border:

1. Cut 10 strips 1-1/4" wide for nine patches.

2. Cut 6 strips 7-5/8" wide. Cut these strips into 26 squares 7-5/8", then cut these squares with an X to yield the 104 quarter-square triangles needed.

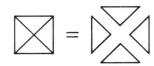

3. Mark 81 squares in a 3-1/8" grid, 9 across by 9 down, to yield 162 triangle units.

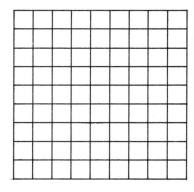

4. Cut 2 squares 4" diagonally in one direction to yield 4 half-square triangles.

Bright accent

1. Cut 12 strips 1-1/4" wide for nine patches.
2. Cut 5 strips 1-1/4" wide for corner nine patches.
3. Cut 12 strips 1-1/4" wide for rails.
4. Cut 16 strips 1-1/4" wide for setting rails.
5. Cut 10 strips 2-1/4" wide for first border.

For pieced border:

Cut 8 strips 1-1/4" wide for nine patches.

Main dark

1. Cut and set aside 1 yd. This fabric will be sewn with light fabric for fast triangles.
2. Cut 2 strips 20-1/2" wide. Cut these strips into 3 squares 20-1/2", then cut these with an X to yield the 10 setting triangles needed.

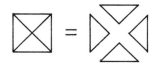

40

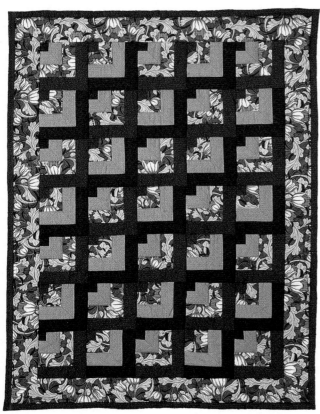

These marvelous quilts, sewn in dramatic colors, machine-piece quickly and easily using the Template-Free™ method. The crib size Strip Rail, left, 32½" x 44½", alternates two blocks that are made from the same set of strips.

The lap size Strip Rail, below, 44½" x 66½", is executed in Amish fabrics for a bold look.

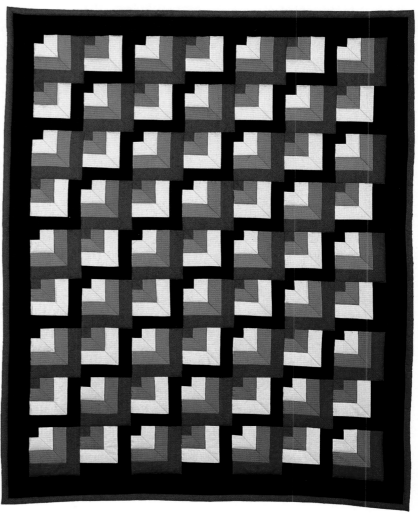

41

Chimneys and Cornerstones, 87''x 105'', is easily cut with the rotary cutter, then machine pieced. Adapted from a traditional pattern and embellished with a pieced border, it will make an excellent addition to your quilt collection.

This scrap quilt, called Scrap-aholic, uses random scraps in just two shapes, squares and triangles. It gives you great practice in cutting and piecing, while allowing you to use up those treasures of scraps. This quilt uses a barnraising set to unify the blocks into a 90" x 105" design with a pieced border.

The crib size Scrap-aholic, 36'' x 51'', makes use of a consistent black square in the center of each block.

This Chimneys and Cornerstones lap quilt, 49'' x 67'', is a beautiful example of an old pattern with a contemporary look. It gives you the additional challenge of adding a pieced border.

A wonderful use of color, this Road to Oklahoma quilt, 48" x 68", features a unique combination of background fabrics to form a delightful design using just one pieced block, in three different colorations.

Pinwheel in Pinwheels, 47'' x 63'', combines large and small pinwheel blocks inside a pieced border. The paisley fabric sets the tone of this restful color scheme.

This brown and rust Goose in the Pond quilt, 87" x 106", was inspired by Marsha McCloskey's quilt from her book **Christmas Quilts.** This quilt has been adapted to be cut with the rotary cutter, yet Marsha's bold interpretation of a traditional design is maintained. The pieced border uses part of the block design to add that special touch that attracts attention.

Simple color combinations allow the Farmer's Stepdaughter design to make a statement. The dark background effectively shows off the lighter star design. This 53½'' square wallhanging is sure to warm up your room. Machine-pieced by Trudie Hughes, hand-quilted by Judy Konkol.

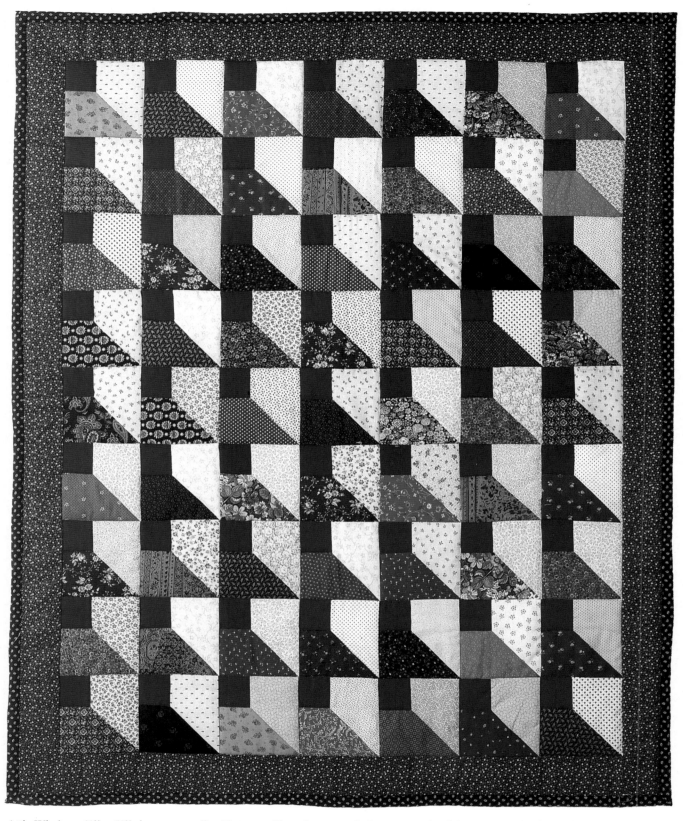

Attic Window, 41" x 51", is a scrap quilt with trapezoids and squares. It features varying light and dark fabrics in the same position.

Flying Geese in the Cabin with its pieced borders is an exciting variation of the Log Cabin. Using trapezoids, triangles, and squares, it provides a challenge for the intermediate quilter. Only one light fabric, four dark fabrics and an accent fabric were used for the large size, 86'' x 104''. The blocks are set in a barnraising design and then framed with a pieced border.

Elnora Schaefer used a pink and blue color scheme for her Flying Geese in the Cabin quilt, 86" x 104".

The lap size of the Flying Geese in the Cabin, 52" x 72", utilizes large black prints on the dark side of the pieced blocks to contrast with the light fabric. The rust accent triangles dramatize the barnraising set.

This Flying Geese in the Cabin, 52" x 72", is a scrap quilt framed with a striped fabric border. Black accent triangles separate the varied light and dark fabrics.

This Christmas Colorado Log Cabin, 45'' x 63'', is a lap quilt which effectively uses Victorian style fabrics to show off the wonderful overall design.

My version of Colorado Log Cabin was inspired by Judy Martin in her book **Scrap Quilts.** The softness of the pastel fabrics and the highlighting of the pieced border make this 91'' x 109'' quilt sparkle.

These Blazing Star wallhangings, 35" square, demonstrate the effective use of color. While the lavender one above uses a light background fabric, the Amish variation uses black for the background.

3. Cut 1 strip 12" wide into 2 squares 12". Cut these once diagonally to yield the corners.

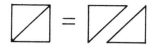

4. Cut 4 strips 1-1/4" wide for nine patches in sashing.
5. Cut 11 strips 2-1/2" wide for last border.
6. Cut 11 strips 2-1/2" wide for binding.

For pieced border:

Cut and set aside 1 yd. to be sewn with light fabric for fast triangles.

Accent dark

1. Cut 32 strips 1-1/4" wide for setting rails.
2. Cut 10 strips 3-1/2" wide for second border.

Piecing and Assembly

Each pieced block measures 11-1/4" and looks like this:

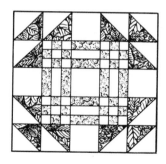

The lattice strips that set this quilt are also pieced.

1. Place light fabric that was marked for fast triangles right sides together with main fabric. Stitch a 1/4" seam down each side of drawn diagonal lines. Cut apart and press.
2. Make 72 nine patches for blocks that look like this:

3. Make 31 nine patches for lattice strips that look like this:

4. Make 72 rail units for blocks that look like this:

2-3/4"

Piece 3 strips for rails. Subcut at 2-3/4" intervals.

5. Make 18 blocks that look like this:

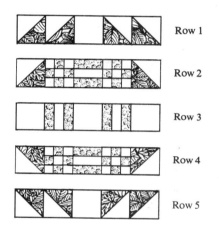

Row 1
Row 2
Row 3
Row 4
Row 5

Assemble blocks in rows.

6. Make 48 setting rail units that look like this:

11-3/4"

Piece 3 strips for setting rails. Subcut at 11-3/4" intervals.

7. Piece the 18 blocks in rows, alternating with setting rail units.

8. Set into diagonal rows, carefully adding setting triangles at end of each row. Alternate setting rails with setting nine patches, following illustration. Add these between rows.

9. For corners, add triangles cut from 12" squares. These are too large, but sew them on anyway.

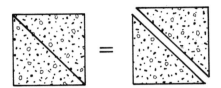

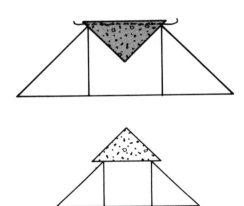

10. Using your plastic triangle, square off corner with sides of quilt. The corner will be square and will lie flat.

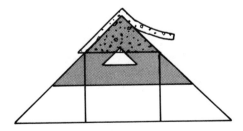

11. Sew on first and second borders, measuring proper lengths and matching centers and ends of border strips with quilt.

CREATIVE OPTION

After sewing on first and second borders, you may add this pieced border.

1. Make 54 units that look like this:

2. Sew units together with quarter-square triangles of light fabric. You will need 2 border strips containing 11 units and 2 border strips containing 14 units.

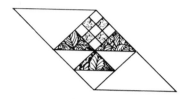

3. Sew half-square triangles on ends of long sides. First, add these borders to quilt, carefully matching centers and ends.

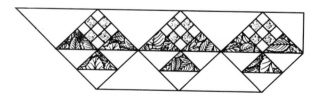

4. Then, sew top and bottom border strips onto quilt matching centers and ends.

5. Make 4 corner units that look like this:

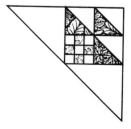

6. Add corners to quilt.

7. Add last border.

Quilts Made with "Decapitated Triangles"

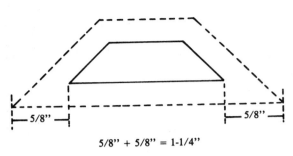

5/8" + 5/8" = 1-1/4"

How to Cut "Decapitated Triangles"

Although this shape is really a trapezoid, I refer to it as a "decapitated triangle" to help you form a mental picture of the shape you will need to cut. These shapes remind me of a quarter-square triangle with its tip cut off. The math is the same: measure the long side and add 1-1/4".

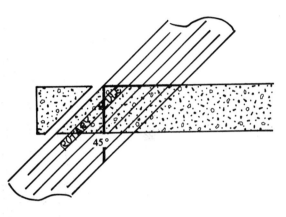

Using the Rotary Rule, align the 45° angle marking with top edge of strip. Cut.

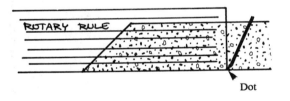

Measure along edge of strip until you get to desired long side plus 1-1/4" seam allowance. Mark.

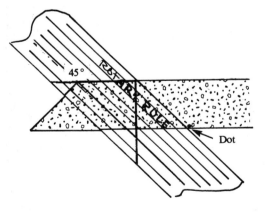

Line up ruler with dot and cut a 45° angle in opposite direction.

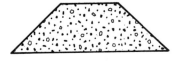

Point is then established for next cut.

Farmer's Stepdaughter

Wallhanging (pictured on page 48)

4 pieced blocks, set diagonally 2 blocks by 2 blocks
Piecing area finishes to approximately 42-1/2'' square.
After first border, quilt will be 44-1/2''.
After pieced border, quilt will be 50-1/2''.
After last border, quilt will be 53-1/2''.

Fabric Requirements:

Dark background—2-3/4 yds. (2 yds. for piecing, 1/2 yd. for last border, 1/4 yd. for pieced border)

Light—1-1/2 yds. (3/4 yd. for piecing, 3/4 yd. for pieced border)

Accent—1-1/2 yds. (1/3 yd. for piecing, 1/3 yd. for first border, 1/2 yd. for binding, 1/3 yd. for pieced border)

Backing—3-1/2 yds.

Cutting Requirements

Background

1. Cut 1 strip 2'' wide for nine-patches.
2. Cut 4 strips 2'' wide. Cut into 32 decapitated triangles, marking points at 5-3/4''. (See page 60 for more details on cutting these.)

3. Cut 2 strips 3-1/2'' wide into 16 rectangles 3-1/2'' by 5''. Using the 1-1/2'' Speedy, take all four corners off rectangles. (See page 65 for instructions on using the Speedy.)

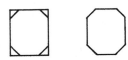

4. Cut 2 strips 3-1/2'' wide into 4 squares 3-1/2'' and 16 rectangles 3-1/2'' by 2''.
5. Cut 1 strip 2'' wide into 16 squares.
6. Cut 1 square 15-1/2''.
7. Cut 1 square 22-1/2''. Cut this square with an X to yield 4 setting triangles.

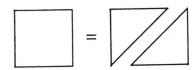

8. Cut 2 squares 12-1/2'' once diagonally for corners of quilt.

9. Cut 6 strips 2'' wide for last border.

For pieced border:

1. Cut 2 strips 3-3/8'' wide. Cut strips into 23 squares, then cut these with an X to yield 92 quarter-square triangles for outside of pieced border.

2. Cut 2 squares 1-7/8'' and cut once diagonally for triangles in corner blocks.

Light

1. Cut 4 strips 2'' wide for nine-patches.
2. Cut 4 strips 2-3/8'' wide into squares. Cut these squares once diagonally to yield 128 triangles. It would help if these were nubbed at 2''. (See page 66 to nub triangles.)

For pieced border:

1. Cut 6 strips 2'' wide. Cut these into 72 rectangles 2'' by 3-1/2''.
2. Cut 1 strip 2'' wide into 4 decapitated triangles, measuring along the cut edge at 5-3/4'' intervals.

3. Cut 2 strips 2'' wide. Fold right sides together (to create mirror images when cut) and cut 16 trapezoids, measuring along cut edge at 3-7/8'' intervals.

4. Cut 4 squares 2''.

Accent

1. Cut 4 strips 2" wide for nine patches.
2. Cut 5 strips 1-1/2" wide for first border.
3. Cut 6 strips 2-1/2" wide for binding.

For pieced border:

1. Cut 2 strips 3-3/8" wide. Cut these into squares, then cut with an X to yield 80 quarter-square triangles.

2. Cut 1 strip 1-7/8" wide into 6 squares. Cut these squares once diagonally to yield 12 triangles.

Piecing and Assembly

One 15" block looks like this:

1. Make 3 sets of 3 sewn strips for nine patches. Cut into 2" segments. Sew into 3 rows, making 16 nine-patch blocks. (See page 8 for information on making nine-patches.)

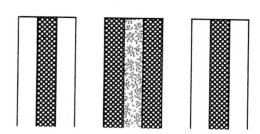

2. Sew triangles onto corners of decapitated triangles and to corners of rectangles that had their corners removed.

3. Assemble this block in rows:

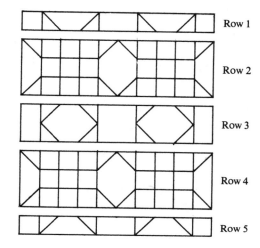

Row 1
Row 2
Row 3
Row 4
Row 5

4. Join larger blocks with large plain square and setting triangles to form rows of quilt. Make sure to accurately sew setting triangles onto ends of each row.

Join rows, then add corners last. (See page 58 for information about sewing on corners.)

5. Sew on first border, measuring proper lengths and matching centers and ends of border strips with quilt.

CREATIVE OPTION

After adding the first border, you may add a pieced border to this quilt. This pieced border is basically made up of 2 units, one being the reverse of the other.

1. Make 36 A units that look like this:

2. Make 36 B units that look like this:

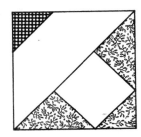

3. Make 4 corner units that look like this:

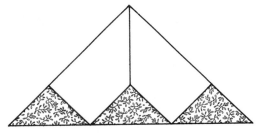

4. Make 4 center turning units that look like this:

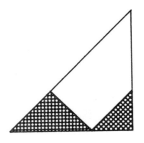

5. Make 4 border ends that look like this:

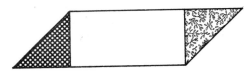

6. Make 4 border ends that look like this:

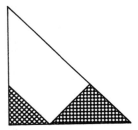

7. Onto one side of each center turning unit, attach 9 A units. Onto the other side of each center turning unit, attach 9 B units.

8. Add 2 border ends to each border strip.

9. Add corners to both ends of 2 border strips.

10. Sew the 2 shorter pieced border strips to opposite sides of quilt.

11. Sew the 2 pieced border strips with corners to other sides of quilt.

12. Sew on last border.

Using the Speedy

If we think of the Snowball block as a square with the corners cut off, we can cut off the right amount with the rotary cutter. To know how much to cut off, we will be making a cutting guide. This guide looks like a template, but is not used as one. I refer to this guide as a SPEEDY.

The Snowball cutting guide is made by drawing the finished triangle that will be sewn onto the corners, adding the seam allowance along the two shorter edges, and removing 1/4'' from the diagonal edge.

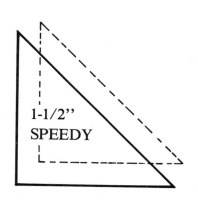

1-1/2''
SPEEDY

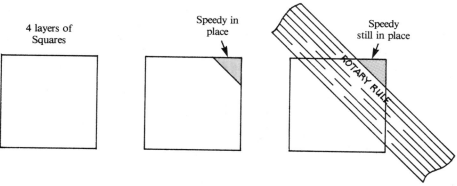

4 layers of Squares

Speedy in place

Speedy still in place

Speedy removed for cutting

Speedy

To know which SPEEDY to use, determine the size of the triangle that will be sewn back on. If you are adding a 2'' triangle, then use the 2'' SPEEDY, and so on.

By having the control gained by cutting off the corners, you can determine how many corners are cut off. Sometimes only 2 or 3 corners will be removed.

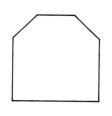

This technique can also be used with other shapes. For the Farmer's Stepdaughter Wallhanging, corners are removed from rectangles.

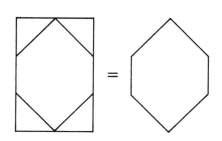

The Rotary Mate™ is a new ruler that makes this step even easier. It contains 4 sizes of Speedies. Just line up ruler with fabric to use.

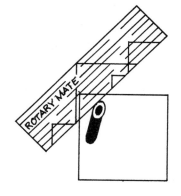

Nubbing

To ensure accurate piecing, I nub the shape to be sewn on. Without nubbing, it is hard to match shapes accurately.

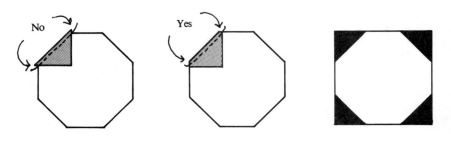

When nubbed, they fit perfectly, Here is a simple way to nub loose triangles:

Stack several of these triangles together. Using a ruler, measure finished size of triangle plus 1/2''. Then cut off excess. Do this on both points.

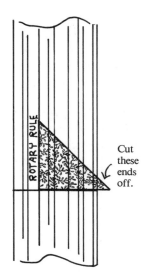

In the Flying Geese in The Cabin pattern, it helps to nub the even numbered trapezoids. Using the long sides of the ruler, cut trapezoids the finished measurement of the long side plus 1/2''.

Quilts Made with Trapezoids

How to Cut Trapezoids

In making quilts with the kind of trapezoid shown here, I discovered that the same math used for half-square triangles also could be used for these trapezoids. Simply add 7/8'' to the length of the long side. Cut strips the width of trapezoid plus seam allowances.

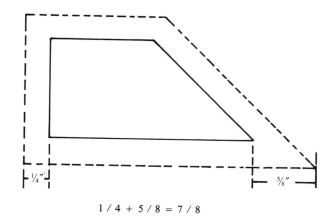

1 / 4 + 5 / 8 = 7 / 8

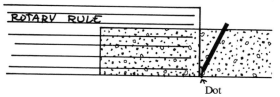

Measure and mark the finished size plus 7/8''.

Working with 4 layers (right sides of fabric facing up), cut left edge perpendicular with top and bottom edges. From left edge, measure finished edge of long side plus 7/8''. Cut again with 45° mark on ruler. It does make a difference where you begin; the point of the trapezoid will go in one direction if you begin at top cut edge and in opposite direction if you begin at bottom cut edge.

You should notice whether the design has just one shape trapezoid or mirror image trapezoid shapes. In some of the patterns, I have instructed you to begin measuring from either top edge or bottom edge. These trapezoids will all be the same with no mirror images. In some designs, it is the right side that has the point, in some the left side.

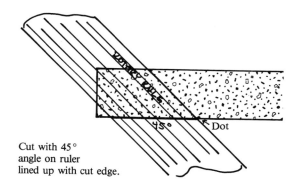

Cut with 45° angle on ruler lined up with cut edge.

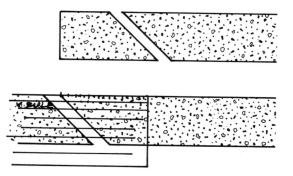

The next cut does not have to be marked. Measure the desired amount and make a straight cut.

Start with the right sides of your fabric strips facing up. If you begin measuring along bottom cut edge and cut with a 45° angle, all your trapezoids will have the point on the right side.

You will measure and mark a dot on every other cut. For second cut, measure the top edge and make a straight cut.

If you begin measuring along top cut edge, and cut with a 45° angle, all your trapezoids will have the point on the left side.

The second cut does not have to be marked. Measure the bottom edge and make a straight cut.

In designs such as "Flying Geese in the Cabin" on page 73, it is important to cut an entire strip the same way. I have tried to indicate whether you are to begin measuring at top or bottom. However, in the pieced border where trapezoids will be going in both directions, I instruct you to take your strips and fold them over once, right sides together, and cut. This will result in mirror image trapezoids.

Attic Window

This quilt appeared in my last book, but no pattern was given. It is a scrap quilt that uses both light and dark fabrics. There are 2 shapes in this quilt: a square and a trapezoid. The trapezoids used are in mirror images. The dark fabrics have their points going in one direction and the light fabrics have their points going in the opposite direction.

The center square in each block should be consistent. To get the optical illusion effect, these squares are best cut from a very dark solid color, such as black, navy, or forest green.

Crib Quilt (pictured on page 49)

63 pieced blocks, set 7 blocks by 9 blocks
Piecing area finishes to 35" by 45".
After borders, quilt will be 41" by 51".

69

Fabric Requirements

Dark centers—1/4 yd. for crib size
1/3 yd. for lap size
1-1/2 yds. for large size

Light—1-1/4 yds. of assorted prints for crib size
(Start with at least 12 different ones. The larger the quilt, the more variety you will need.)
2 yds. of assorted prints for lap size
4-1/2 yds. of assorted prints for large size

Dark—Same as light

Border—3/4 yd. for crib size
1 yd. for lap size
1-1/4 yds. for large size

Binding—1/2 yd. for crib size
3/4 yd. for lap size
1 yd. for large size

Backing—1-3/4 yds. for crib size
4 yds. for lap size
6-1/2 yds. for large size

Cutting Requirements

Dark centers

Cut 2-1/2" wide strips into squares. You will need one per block.

Dark and Light Scraps

1. Cut 3-1/2" wide strips from several light and dark fabrics. I try to cut at least 6 layers at a time. These strips need not be the entire width of the fabric. Since variety is most important, you do not want too many trapezoids of any one fabric.

2. Stack 3 layers of dark fabric right sides up, then 3 layers of light fabric right sides down. This will give you dark trapezoids that are the mirror images of the light ones.

3. Straighten left edge and measure along bottom cut edge at 5-7/8" intervals and make a dot. Line up 45° line on ruler with cut edge of strips, stopping just short of dot, and cut. The next cut will be measured along top. Starting with the point, measure 5-7/8" and make a straight cut. You will need to make a mark only every other cut. Since you are cutting many layers at a time, this is a fast quilt to cut.

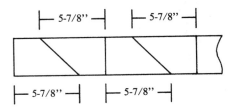

Borders

1. Cut 5 strips 3-1/2" wide for crib size.
2. Cut 7 strips 3-1/2" wide for lap size.
3. Cut 10 strips 3-1/2" wide for large size.

Binding

1. Cut 5 strips 2-1/2" wide for crib size.
2. Cut 7 strips 2-1/2" wide for lap size.
3. Cut 10 strips 2-1/2" wide for large size.

Piecing and Assembly

One 5" block looks like this:

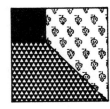

1. This is like mitering a corner. Begin with small square on top of dark trapezoid. Stitch from bottom, stop 1/4" from end, and backstitch here.

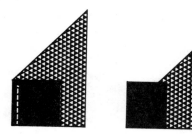

2. Next, line up square with light trapezoid. Stitch from bottom and stop 1/4" from end. This will be the same spot the last stitching ended. These 2 stitching lines should meet, but not go beyond their intersection.

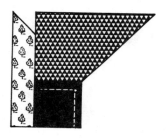

3. Then, line up points and sew, matching from outside to corner intersection again. Press all seams away from center square.

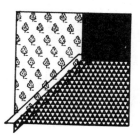

4. Sew blocks in rows.

5. Add borders.

Lap Quilt (not pictured)

108 pieced blocks, set 9 blocks by 12 blocks
Piecing area finishes to 45" by 60".
After borders, quilt will be 51" by 66".

Large Quilt (not pictured)

280 pieced blocks, set 14 blocks by 20 blocks
Piecing area finishes to 70" by 100".
After borders, quilt will be 76" by 106".

Flying Geese in the Cabin

Large Quilt (pictured on page 50)

Flying Geese in the Cabin

Large Quilt (pictured on page 50)

48 pieced blocks, set 6 blocks by 8 blocks
Piecing area finishes to 60" by 80".
After first border, quilt will be 64" by 84".
After second border, quilt will be 72" by 90".
After pieced border, quilt will be 80" by 98".
After last border, quilt will be 86" by 104".

Fabric Requirements

Light—2-3/4 yds.
Accent—3-1/4 yds. (1-3/4 yds. for piecing, 3/4 yd. for pieced border, 3/4 yd. for first border)
First dark—1-1/4 yds. (1/2 yd. for piecing, 3/4 yd. for pieced border)
Second dark—3-3/4 yds. (3/4 yds. for piecing, 3 yds. for second and last borders)
Third dark—1 yd.
Fourth dark—3-1/4 yds. (1-1/4 yds. for piecing, 1 yd. for pieced border, 1 yd. for binding)
Backing—9-3/4 yds. (the extra width could be used for second and last borders)

Cutting Requirements

Light

1. Cut 58 strips 1-1/2" wide. Measure along cut edge at 2-7/8", 3-7/8", 4-7/8", 5-7/8", 6-7/8", 7-7/8", 8-7/8", and 9-7/8" intervals. Begin measuring even numbered cuts, i.e. 2-7/8", 4-7/8", etc., along bottom edge and odd numbered cuts, i.e. 3-7/8", 5-7/8", etc., along top edge. Cut 48 trapezoids of each length.

NOTE: Since dark and light fabrics will be cut the same in each round, layer strips with all right sides facing up, cutting at least 2 dark layers and 2 light layers at one time. Cut all the same lengths together. (Refer to page 67 for more details on cutting these trapezoids.)

Accent

1. Cut 3 strips 2-1/2" wide into 48 squares for block centers.
2. Cut 14 strips 2-7/8" wide into 192 squares, then cut squares once diagonally into 384 triangles. Nub them at 2-1/2" from perpendicular cuts. (See page 66 for information on nubbing.)

3. Cut 9 strips 2-1/2" wide for first border.

For pieced border:

1. Cut 7 strips 2-3/8" wide into 108 squares, then cut these once diagonally into 216 triangles.
2. Cut 4 squares 3".

First dark

Cut 7 strips 1-1/2" wide. Cut 48 trapezoids at 2-7/8" intervals, beginning measurement along bottom edge. Cut 48 trapezoids at 3-7/8" intervals, beginning measurement along top edge.

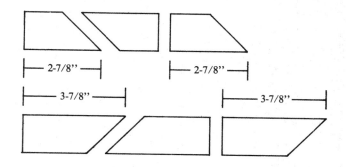

For pieced border:

Cut 11 strips 2" wide. Alternate right and wrong sides of these strips, so you can cut 108 trapezoids with points going in both directions. Measure along cut edge at 4-7/8" intervals and make cuts.

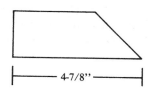

Second dark

1. Cut 11 strips 1-1/2" wide. Cut 48 trapezoids at 4-7/8" intervals, beginning measurement along bottom edge. Cut 48 trapezoids at 5-7/8" intervals beginning measurement along top edge.

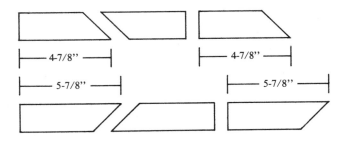

2. From length of fabric, cut 6 strips 4-1/2" wide and 2 strips 4" wide for borders.

Third dark

Cut 16 strips 1-1/2" wide. Cut 48 trapezoids at 6-7/8" intervals, beginning measurement along bottom edge. Cut 48 trapezoids at 7-7/8" intervals, beginning measurement along top edge.

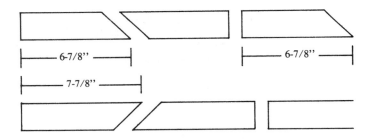

Fourth dark

1. Cut 24 strips 1-1/2" wide. Cut 48 trapezoids at 8-7/8" intervals, beginning measurement at bottom edge. Cut 48 trapezoids at 9-7/8" intervals, beginning measurement along top edge.

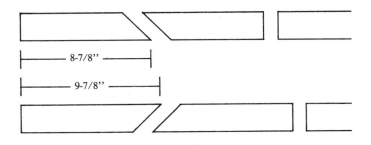

2. Cut 11 strips 2-1/2" wide for binding.

For pieced border:

Cut 12 strips 2" wide. Alternate the direction of right sides of these strips, so you can cut 116 trapezoids with points going in both directions. Measure along cut edge at 4-7/8" intervals and make cuts.

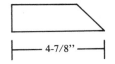

Piecing and Assembly

Each 10" pieced block is made up of a center square, trapezoids, and triangles. It looks like this:

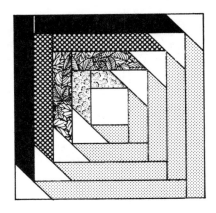

Although this block looks like a log cabin block, it is not pieced like one. It is pieced in rounds.

1. Sew one light strip and one first dark strip onto opposite sides of center square. You might want to nub these beginning trapezoids. Place long side along ruler and line up the 2 perpendicular sides with 2-1/2" mark. Cut small tip off.

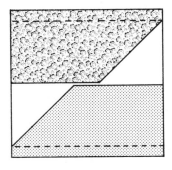

Hint: It helps to nub all even numbered trapezoids. This will give you a guide at the beginning of each round to keep your blocks accurate. See page 66.

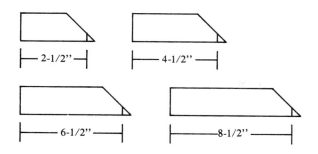

- 2-1/2"
- 4-1/2"
- 6-1/2"
- 8-1/2"

2. Add one length of light and one length of first dark onto other 2 sides. Be sure to have points intersecting at 1/4", leaving only 1/4" seam allowance at corners.

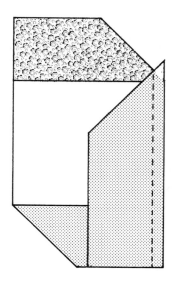

1/4" seam allowance remaining

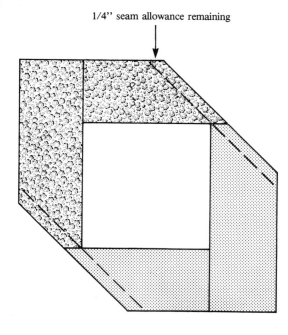

3. Sew nubbed triangles onto missing corners.

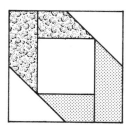

4. Proceed in same manner with next round of light and second dark. Work around until all 10" squares are pieced.

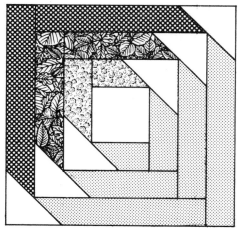

5. Sew blocks into rows and join rows, using a barnraising setting.

6. Sew on first border, then second border, measuring proper lengths and matching centers and ends of border strips with quilt.
NOTE: The second border will be 3" finished for top and bottom but 4" finished for sides. This will make the pieced border mathematically compatible.

CREATIVE OPTION

After adding first and second borders to quilt top, you may add this pieced border. It is made up of 2 units, one being the reverse of the other.

1.   Make 54 A units that look like this:

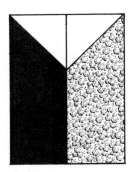

Sew a triangle onto pointed end of each trapezoid. Press seams toward trapezoid on first dark fabric and toward triangle on fourth dark fabric. Having seam allowances pressed in opposite directions will make it easier to match intersections.

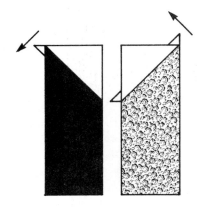

2.   Make 54 B units that look like this:

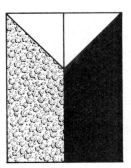

3.   Make 4 corner units that look like this:

4.   Sew 2 strips of 12 A units in a row and 2 strips of 12 B units in a row. Join an A strip to a B strip. Sew these border strips to top and bottom of quilt, matching centers and ends.

5.   Sew 2 strips of 15 A units in a row and 2 strips of 15 B units in a row. Join an A strip to a B strip. Attach corner units to each end of these border strips, then sew to quilt, matching centers and ends.

6.   Sew on last border.

QUILTING TIP: I found it easier to first quilt in the seams that would break the quilt into rows in both directions. Next, I went around center squares, then 2 logs out.

Lap Quilt (pictured on page 52)

24 pieced blocks, set 4 blocks by 6 blocks
Piecing area finishes to 40" by 60".
After first border, quilt will be 44" by 64".
After pieced border, quilt will be 50" by 70".
After last border, quilt will be 54" by 74".

Fabric Requirements

Light—1-3/4 yds. (1-1/4 yds. for piecing, 1/2 yd. for pieced border)
Accent—1-1/2 yds. (1 yd. for piecing, 1/2 yd. for first border)
First dark—1 yd. (1/4 yd. for piecing, 3/4 yd. for pieced border)
Second dark—1/3 yd.
Third dark—1-1/4 yds. (1/2 yd. for piecing, 3/4 yd. for pieced border)
Fourth dark—1-1/3 yds. (5/8 yds. for piecing, 2/3 yd. for last border)
Backing—3-1/2 yds. (pieced crosswise)

Cutting Requirements

Light

Cut 30 strips 1-1/2'' wide. Measure along cut edge at 2-7/8'', 3-7/8'', 4-7/8'', 5-7/8'', 6-7/8'', 7-7/8'', 8-7/8'', and 9-7/8'' intervals. Remember to measure even numbers along bottom and and odd numbers along top. (See page 67 for more details on cutting these trapezoids.) Cut 24 trapezoids of each length.

For pieced border:

1. Cut 6 strips 1-7/8'' wide into 108 squares. Cut these diagonally to yield 216 triangles.

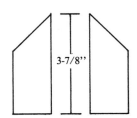

2. Cut 1 strip 1-1/2'' wide into 8 trapezoids, measuring along cut edge at 3-7/8'' intervals. Fold strip in half to cut mirror image trapezoids.

Accent

1. Cut 2 strips 2-1/2'' wide into 24 squares for block centers.
2. Cut 8 strips 2-7/8'' wide into 96 squares. Cut these squares once diagonally into 192 triangles. Nub them at 2-1/2'' from perpendicular cuts.

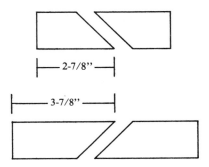

3. Cut 6 strips 2-1/2'' wide for first border.

First dark

Cut 4 strips 1-1/2'' wide. Cut 24 trapezoids at 2-7/8'' intervals, beginning measurement along bottom edge. Cut 24 trapezoids at 3-7/8'' intervals, beginning measurement along top edge.

For pieced border:

1. Cut 15 strips 1-1/2'' wide. Fold each strip in half, layer several folded strips, and cut these strips into 108 trapezoids measuring along cut edge at 3-7/8'' intervals. These trapezoids will be mirror images.

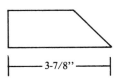

2. Cut 4 squares 2-1/2'' for corner units.

Second dark

Cut 6 strips 1-1/2'' wide. Cut 24 trapezoids at 4-7/8'' intervals, beginning measurement along bottom edge. Cut 24 trapezoids at 5-7/8'' intervals, beginning measurement along top edge.

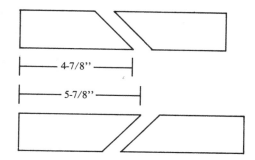

Third dark

Cut 8 strips 1-1/2'' wide. Cut 24 trapezoids at 6-7/8'' intervals, beginning measurement along bottom edge. Cut 24 trapezoids at 7-7/8'' intervals, beginning measurement along top edge.

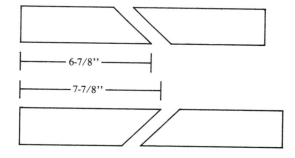

For pieced border:

Cut 15 strips 1-1/2'' wide. Fold each strip in half, layer several folded strips, and cut these strips into 108 trapezoids, measuring along cut edge at 3-7/8'' intervals. These trapezoids will be mirror images.

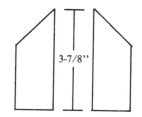

Fourth dark

1. Cut 12 strips 1-1/2'' wide. Cut 24 trapezoids at 8-7/8'' intervals, beginning measurement along bottom edge. Cut 24 trapezoids at 9-7/8'' intervals, beginning measurement along top edge.

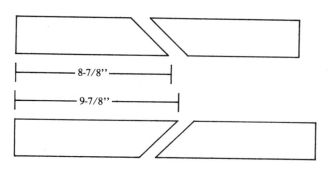

2. Cut 8 strips 2-1/2'' wide for last border.

Piecing and Assembly

1. Follow instructions given for large quilt on page 74. You will need to piece 24 blocks and sew them together in a barnraising setting, 4 blocks by 6 blocks.

2. Sew on first border, measuring proper lengths and matching centers and ends of border strips with quilt.

CREATIVE OPTION

After adding the first border, you may add a pieced border to this quilt.

1. Make 54 A units that look like this:

2. Make 54 B units that look like this:

3. Make 4 corner units that look like this:

4. Sew 2 strips of 11 A units and 2 strips of 11 B units in a row. Join an A strip to a B strip. Sew these border strips to top and bottom of quilt, matching centers and ends.

5. Sew 2 strips of 16 A units and 2 strips of 16 B units in a row. Join an A strip to a B strip. Add corner units onto ends. Sew these border strips to sides, matching corners and ends.

6. Add last border.

Quilts Made with Diamonds

How to Cut Diamonds

When working with a design where one particular fabric has the points consistently going in one direction, layer the strips with the right side always facing up (so you don't cut some reversed pieces). If the design has a reverse of this shape as well, just fold strip so that you will get both the shape and its reverse when you cut.

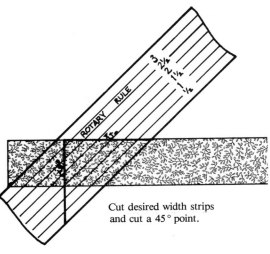

Cut desired width strips and cut a 45° point.

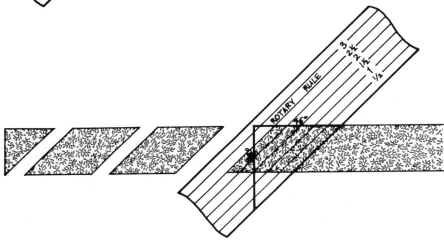

When 2 or more diamonds are to be sewn together, sew strips together and then use a ruler to cut proper angle. It is the same principle as that used in straight cuts.

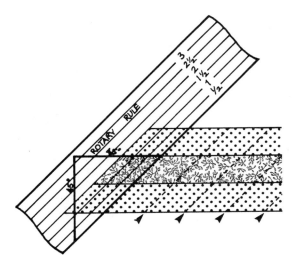

Colorado Log Cabin

Large Quilt (pictured on page 55)

Colorado Log Cabin

This quilt was designed by Judy Martin. When I received Judy's book, *Scrap Quilts*, I immediately began to translate her patterns into usable measurements for the rotary cutter. I fell in love with this quilt and couldn't wait to make it. I have given you instructions here for my version. In adapting this design to the rotary cutter, I changed the size of the block to 9", whereas Judy's original quilt used 12" blocks.

Large Quilt (pictured on page 55)

80 pieced blocks, set 8 blocks by 10 blocks
Piecing area finishes to 72" by 90".
After first border, quilt will be 74" by 92".
After second border, quilt will be 78" by 96".
After pieced border, quilt will be 85" by 103".
After last border, quilt will be 91" by 109".

Fabric Requirements

Light—5-1/4 yds. (4 yds. for piecing, 1-1/4 yds. for pieced border)
Accent—3-3/4 yds. (1-1/2 yds. for piecing, 1/2 yd. for first border, 3/4 yd. for pieced border, 1 yd. for binding) Choose a solid color.
First dark—5/8 yd.
Second dark—1 yd.
Third dark—2-1/4 yds. (1-1/4 yds. for piecing, 1 yd. for second border)
Fourth dark—3-1/2 yds. (1-1/2 yds. for piecing, 3/4 yds. for pieced border, 1-1/4 yds. for last border)
Backing—9-1/2 yds. (One of borders and binding could be taken from sides after 3 lengths are pieced.)

Cutting Requirements

Light

1. Cut 86 strips 1-1/2" wide. From these, cut 160 squares 1-1/2" and 80 rectangles each, of the following lengths: 2-1/2", 3-1/2", 4-1/2", 5-1/2", 6-1/2".

2. Cut 160 decapitated triangles, measuring along cut edge at 7-1/2" intervals. (See page 60 for more details on cutting these.) You should get 5 decapitated triangles per strip.

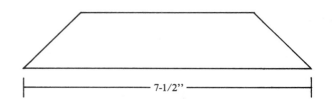

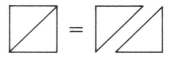

For pieced border:

1. Cut 15 strips 2-3/8" wide into 236 squares. Cut these squares diagonally into 472 triangles.

2. Cut 4 squares 2-1/2" for corners.

Accent

1. Cut 32 strips 1-1/2" wide into 640 diamonds. After establishing first diagonal cut, line up bias edge with 1-1/2" marking on ruler. (See page 80 for more details on cutting these.) You should get 20 diamonds per strip.

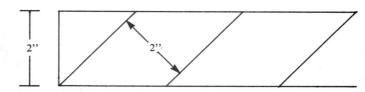

2. Cut 9 strips 1-1/2" wide for first border.
3. Cut 12 strips 2-1/2" wide for binding.

For pieced border:

1. Cut 11 strips 2" wide into 124 diamonds. After establishing first diagonal cut, line up bias cut edge with 2" marking on ruler. You should get 12 diamonds per strip.

First dark

Cut 12 strips 1-1/2" wide. From these, cut 80 rectangles 1-1/2" by 2-1/2" and 80 rectangles 1-1/2" by 3-1/2".

Second dark

1. Cut 20 strips 1-1/2" wide. From these, cut 80 rectangles 1-1/2" by 4-1/2" and 80 rectangles 1-1/2" by 5-1/2".

Third dark

1. Cut 27 strips 1-1/2" wide. From these, cut 80 rectangles 1-1/2" by 6-1/2" and 80 rectangles 1-1/2" wide by 7-1/2".
2. Cut 10 strips 2-1/2" wide for second border.

Fourth dark

1. Cut 32 strips 1-1/2" wide. From these, cut 160 decapitated triangles, measuring along cut edge at 7-1/2" intervals.

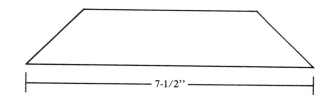

2. Cut 10 strips 3-1/2" wide for last border.

For pieced border:

Cut 10 strips 2" wide into 116 diamonds. After establishing first diagonal cut, line up bias edge with 2" marking on ruler.

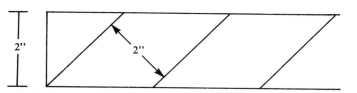

Piecing and Assembly

1. Piece this log cabin block as you would any other log cabin block, starting with light side. Sew 2 logs of light, then 2 logs of dark, then 2 logs of light, etc. Make sure raw edges of logs match.

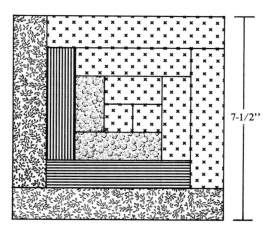

Block should measure 7-1/2" from raw edge to raw edge after third dark fabric is sewn on.

2. To piece the last row: Carefully sew bias sides of diamonds to bias sides of decapitated triangles. DO NOT PRESS THESE UNTIL THEY ARE ADDED TO BLOCK.

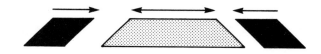

This will result in a straight-of-grain strip to be sewn onto log cabin block.

Begin and end stitching 1/4" from ends.

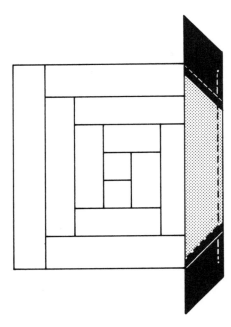

When joining the last row, push seams of diamonds toward you. One will be toward decapitated triangle, the other away. This will help match diamonds when blocks are joined together in rows for quilt.

After all strips have been added, miter corners.

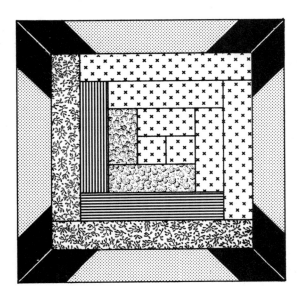

3. Sew these 80 blocks into rows and then into quilt top, using a barnraising setting. When joining blocks you will find the seam allowances of the diamonds are facing in opposite directions. This will help ensure accurate 8-pointed stars.

4. Sew on first border, then second border, measuring proper lengths and matching centers and ends of border strips with quilt.

CREATIVE OPTION

After adding the first border, you may add a pieced border to this quilt. It is made up of 2 units, one being the reverse of the other.

1. Make 58 A blocks that look like this:

Sew a triangle onto each bias edge of diamonds. Press seams toward triangles on third dark fabric and toward diamonds on accent fabric. In this way, seam allowances will be in opposite directions when these are sewn into pairs. This helps match intersections.

2. Make 58 B blocks that look like this:

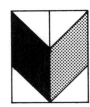

3. Make 4 corner units that look like this:

4. Sew 2 strips of 13 A blocks in a row and 2 strips of 13 B blocks in a row. Join an A strip to a B strip. Sew these border strips to top and bottom of quilt, matching centers and ends.

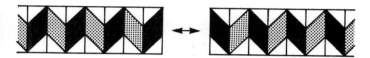

5. Sew 2 strips of 16 A blocks in a row and 2 strips of 16 B blocks in a row. Join an A strip to a B strip. Attach corner units to each end of border strips, then sew to quilt, matching centers and ends.

6. Sew on last border.

QUILTING TIP: I found it easier to define blocks by first machine quilting in all crosswise and lengthwise long seams. Then I came in 2 logs and quilted around, then around center square. It is important to cross stars no more than twice, or they will smash down.

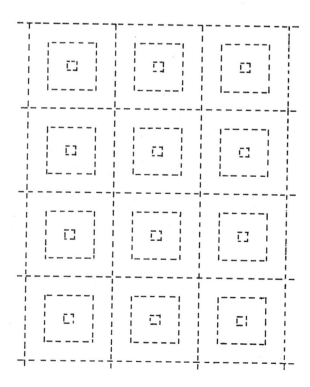

Lap Quilt (pictured on page 54)
24 pieced blocks, set 4 blocks by 6 blocks
Piecing area finishes to 36'' by 54''.
After first border, quilt will be 39'' by 57''.
After last border, quilt will be 45'' by 63''.

Fabric Requirements

Light—1-1/4 yds.
Accent for stars—2 yds. (3/4 yd. for piecing,
             yd. for first border, 3/4 yd. for
             binding)
First dark—1/4 yd.
Second dark—1/3 yd.
Third dark—1-1/4 yds. (1/2 yds. for piecing, 3/4
             yd. for last border)
Fourth dark—5/8 yd.
Center squares—1/8 yd.
Backing—3 yds. (pieced crosswise)

Cutting Requirements

Light

1. Cut 27 strips 1-1/2" wide. From these, cut 24 each, of the following lengths: 1-1/2", 2-1/2", 3-1/2", 4-1/2", 5-1/2", and 6-1/2".

2. Cut 48 decapitated triangles, measuring along cut edge at 7-1/2" intervals. (See page 60 for more details on cutting these.)

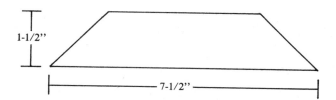

Accent

1. Cut 10 strips 1-1/2" wide into 192 diamonds.

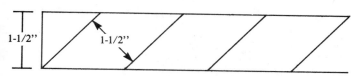

2. Cut 6 strips 2" wide for first border.
3. Cut 7 strips 2-1/2" wide for binding.

First dark

1. Cut 4 strips 1-1/2" wide. From these, cut 24 rectangles 1-1/2" by 2-1/2" and 24 rectangles 1-1/2" by 3-1/2".

Second dark

Cut 6 strips 1-1/2" wide. From these, cut 24 rectangles 1-1/2" by 4-1/2" and 24 rectangles 1-1/2" by 5-1/2".

Third dark

1. Cut 9 strips 1-1/2" wide. From these, cut 24 rectangles 1-1/2" by 6-1/2" and 24 rectangles 1-1/2" by 7-1/2".
2. Cut 7 strips 3-1/2" wide for last border.

Fourth dark

Cut 10 strips 1-1/2" wide. From these, cut 48 decapitated triangles, measuring along cut edge at 7-1/2" intervals.

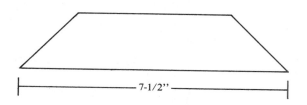

Center squares

Cut 1 strip 1-1/2" wide into 24 squares.

Piecing and Assembly

1. Follow instructions given for large quilt on page 83. You will need to piece 24 blocks and sew them together in a barn-raising setting, 4 blocks by 6 blocks.

2. Add borders.

Blazing Star Wallhanging

This quilt has had the reputation of being difficult to piece. With the rotary cutter and sewing machine, you can streamline your work. You do not need to cut single diamonds, and there is no marking.

This miniature size is easier to tackle, as there is less stretch to the diamonds. You must be careful with seam allowances and matching beginnings and ends of pieces.

Blazing Star Wallhanging (pictured on page 56)

Piecing area finishes to 29" square.
After border, quilt will be 35" square.

Fabric Requirements

To simplify this quilt, work with a background fabric and 4 other fabrics. Shade light to dark, planning either light or dark fabric for the points of the stars, depending on the background fabric. This is a reverse-repeat setup.

Background—2/3 yd.
Fabric 1—1/4 yd.
Fabric 2—1/3 yd.
Fabric 3—1/2 yd.
Fabric 4—1/3 yd.
Binding—1/3 yd.
Border—1/2 yd.
Backing—1 yd.

Cutting Requirements

Background

1. Cut 3 strips 4-3/4" wide into 20 squares.

2. Cut 2 squares 7-1/4". Cut these squares with an X to yield 8 triangles for outside of quilt.

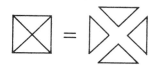

Fabric 1

Cut 4 strips 1-1/4" wide.

Fabric 2

Cut 8 strips 1-1/4" wide.

Fabric 3

Cut 12 strips 1-1/4" wide.

Fabric 4

Cut 8 strips 1-1/4" wide.

Border

Cut 4 strips 3-1/2" wide.

Binding

Cut 4 strips 2-1/2" wide.

Piecing and Assembly

Miniature blazing star needs 32 star points.

1. Make these 2 sets of strips. There are only 2 sets of strips to make. You will need 2 cuts from each set of strips for each star point. One setup of 4 strips sewn together will give you 22 cuts. You will need 4 setups of each set for entire small quilt.

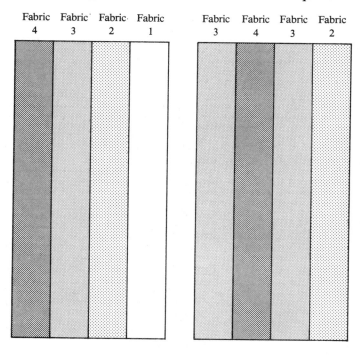

2. To cut them, place 45° line of ruler on a stitching line. The first cut establishes the angle.

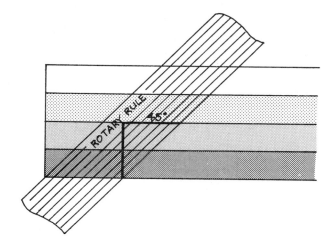

3. Lining bias cut edge of strips with numbers in middle of ruler, make cuts every 1-1/4''.

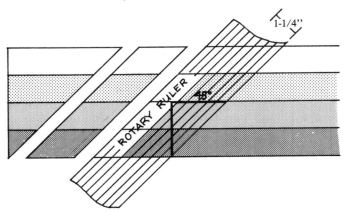

I strongly suggest that the 45° angle be on a stitching line for every cut, as it is very easy to drift, changing the angle.

4. Sew one strip from each setup into pairs. You will need a total of 64 pairs. Tip: You will need to pin each intersection.

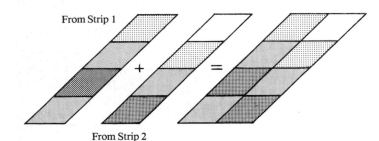

5. Sew 2 pairs into a star point. Make 32 star points.

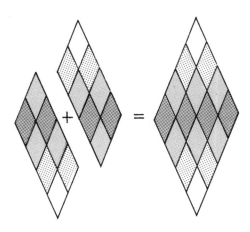

6. Sew star points into 2 groups of 4 and 8 groups of 3. Stop stitching 1/4'' from end of V formed.

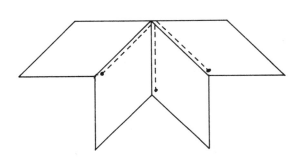

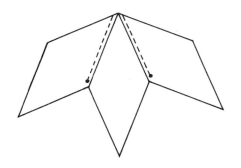

7. Sew the 2 groups of 4 together into center star.

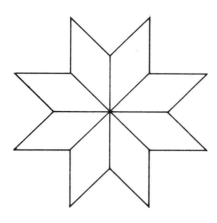

8. Piece a background square into each V formed. Be sure to stop stitching 1/4" from end of each seam.

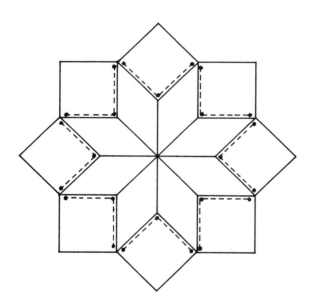

9. Sew a group of 3 star points into each new V formed. Match seams and sew, beginning and ending 1/4" from ends.

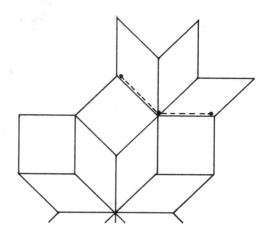

10. Add remaining squares and triangles. Begin and end seams 1/4" from ends.

11. Add border.

Finishing Your Quilt

Borders

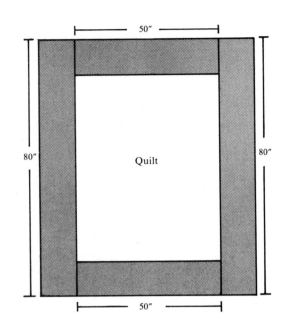

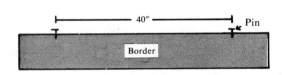

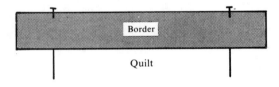

Over the years, I have observed quiltmakers doing wonderful work piecing their quilts, only to undo it when they put the borders on. Many people just take a strip of fabric and sew it on the edge of their quilt and then cut it off. Many times they put different amounts on each time they sew, creating real problems.

When the borders have been sewn on, opposite sides of a quilt should measure the same. To ensure this, measure the quilt before adding the borders, and precut borders to match quilt. If you are not mitering, you can cut them accurately, matching them to quilt at each end and middle, then sewing them on. Start with 2 opposite sides and then the other 2 sides.

Many of the patterns in this book have the creative option of a pieced border. These are always preceded by a first border. It is this first border that makes the pieced border mathematically compatible to the quilt. I find it easier to keep the quilt squared by blunting borders instead of mitering them. Carefully measure plain borders, match beginnings, ends, and centers and sew on accurately. If you choose not to add a pieced border, you can sew on last border directly to first border, but, of course, the quilt will be smaller.

Layering and Quilting

Nothing can replace the wonderful look of hand quilting. However, it is not the best choice for all quilts and is very time-consuming. If you are simply outlining your piecing, why not do it on the machine?

Crib quilts and heavily used quilts, which will be washed over and over, are ideal choices to machine quilt. The more you quilt on the machine, the more comfortable you will become. Most of the quilts in this book have been machine quilted. Some include freehand quilting, using a darning foot on the machine. The following tips will enable you to quilt with any standard sewing machine.

Measure your quilt. The back and batting should be 2" to 3" larger than the finished top on all sides. Backings cut from busy prints are ideal for machine quilting. Actual stitches do not show; you see only the outline of the design. For inexperienced machine quilters, these prints help to conceal work that is "less than perfect."

The backing may be pieced with horizontal or vertical seams; they won't be seen once it is quilted. Just before layering, give it one last pressing to remove any remaining fold lines and to ensure that the seaming is flat.

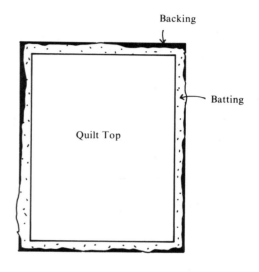

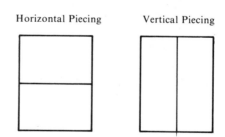

Horizontal Piecing   Vertical Piecing

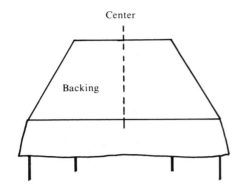

Center

Backing

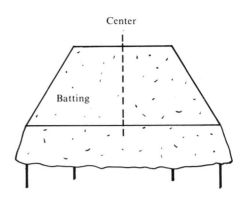

Center

Batting

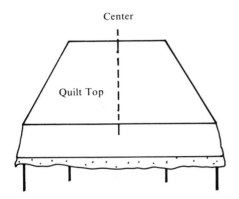

Center

Quilt Top

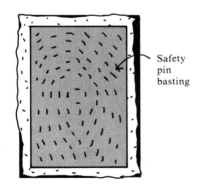

Safety pin basting

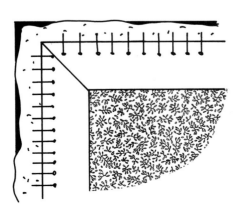

Lay out backing for your quilt on a table, wrong side up. The floor is not a good choice, since you usually have to crawl onto it, and things will surely shift. Use a table pad to protect your dining room table. A ping pong table or long table also works well.

Spread your batting over the backing; smooth and pull out any remaining folds.

Place quilt on top, centering it on backing. Check all four sides to see that there is adequate backing and batting. Reach under batting and tug backing to pull out any waves made by layering. If you don't, you may quilt in tucks. Smooth out top with your hands, checking for any odd bumps from either batting or backing.

Baste quilt with safety pins. A size 2 safety pin works well. It is large enough to catch all layers, but is not so large that it makes big holes in the quilt. More and more quilt shops are carrying these. This system works for hand quilting as well. The safety pin method of basting holds the layers secure. There isn't the play in the layers that you often find in hand basting. There are no threads to snag and pull out, and the speed in assembling is wonderful. The pinning should be at frequent intervals. Every 4'' is not too close together. You should not be able to put your hand down without touching a pin. The more you put in, the easier it is to handle your quilt. I put a quilt on my 17-year-old son's bed before I could find time to quilt it and he wondered about the pins. I told him it was a "punk" quilt and he snuggled right under it. One of my students said her mother-in-law asked if quilters were doing that now instead of tying those little bows. The pins are bound to cause comments from those who have never seen safety pin basting.

Straight pin outside edge perpendicular to edge of quilt at about 1-1/2'' intervals. As soon as the inside of your quilt is secured, the outside wants to flip up and ripple. This fluff must be held in place.

94

Binding

At this time I go ahead and bind my quilts. Since I feel very secure with the safety pin basting, I finish the edge so that the batting does not interfere with the machine quilting. I use straight bindings rather than bias to make larger, fatter bindings. On large quilts, these look like piping. Bindings can be single or double layered. If you want only one layer, cut binding strips 2-1/2" to 3" wide. For double layered bindings, cut binding strips 5-1/2" wide. Binding strips are cut cross-grain and pieced together at a slant (like the borders).

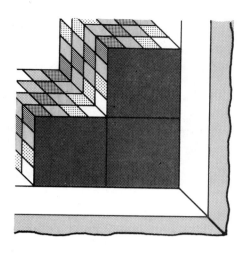

All the quilt patterns in this book give you the number of strips needed for single bindings. Be sure to increase the yardage purchased to cut wider strips for double bindings.

Even if I do not miter all borders, I miter my bindings. It makes for a more pleasing corner. Sew the bindings on through all layers.

Remove the straight pins, miter the corners, and trim excess backing (not the batting) away about 1/4" from the stitching you just completed.

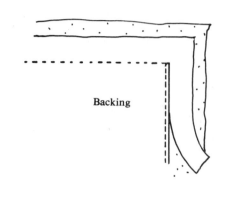

Open the binding out and trim the batting even with that outside edge. This excess batting will be folded in when the binding is brought to the back.

Even though I do everything else on the machine, I prefer to finish the bindings on the quilt back by hand. For gently rounded bindings, turn under 1/4" of the raw edge and bring that fold just past the stitching line on the back. Sew with an applique stitch or blind stitch. This stitching should not be visible.

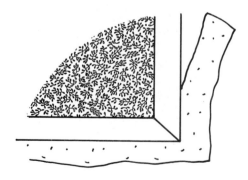

Handling the Corners

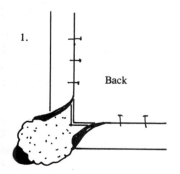

1.

Back

Pin from both directions.

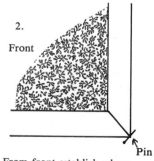

2.

Front

Pin

From front establish where corner will turn. Place a pin.

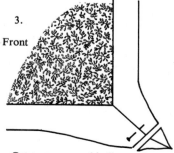

3.

Front

Cut away excess binding and batting 1/4" away from pin.

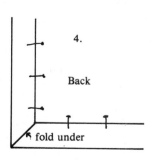

4.

Back

fold under

About the Author

Trudie Hughes, who is also the author of **Template-Free™ Quiltmaking,** has taught quilting for ten years. In addition to teaching in her home state of Wisconsin, she has taught and lectured throughout the United States and in England and France. Her experience also has prompted her to invent two rulers for the rotary cutter.

Currently the owner of a quilt shop, Patched Works, Trudie admits to being an avid fabric-aholic. She has quilted all her adult life, and quilts are constantly on her mind. She lives in Elm Grove, Wisconsin and drives a little red sports car.

The ROTARY RULE™ and ROTARY MATE™ are available through Patched Works, 13330 Watertown Plank Rd., Elm Grove, Wisconsin 53122.

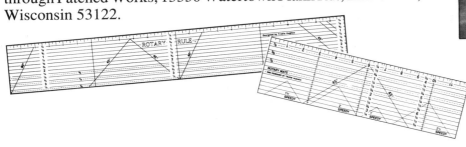

That Patchwork Place Publications

Angelsong by Joan Vibert
Angle Antics by Mary Hickey
Baby Quilts from Grandma by Carolann Palmer
Back to Square One by Nancy J. Martin
A Banner Year by Nancy J. Martin
Basket Garden by Mary Hickey
Blockbuster Quilts by Margaret J. Miller
Calendar Quilts by Joan Hanson
Cathedral Window: A Fresh Look by Nancy J. Martin
Christmas Memories—A Folk Art Celebration
        by Nancy J. Martin
Copy Art for Quilters by Nancy J. Martin
A Dozen Variables by Marsha McCloskey and Nancy J. Martin
Even More by Trudie Hughes
Fit To Be Tied by Judy Hopkins
Handmade Quilts by Mimi Dietrich
Happy Endings—Finishing the Edges of Your Quilt
        by Mimi Dietrich
Holiday Happenings by Christal Carter
Home for Christmas by Nancy J. Martin and Sharon Stanley
Lessons in Machine Piecing by Marsha McCloskey
Little by Little by Mary Hickey
My Mother's Quilts: Designs from the Thirties by Sara Nephew
Ocean Waves by Marsha McCloskey and Nancy J. Martin
One-of-a-Kind Quilts by Judy Hopkins
Pieces of the Past by Nancy J. Martin

Pineapple Passion by Nancy Smith and Lynda Milligan
Quilts to Share by Janet Kime
Red and Green: An Appliqué Tradition by Jeana Kimball
Reflections of Baltimore by Jeana Kimball
Scrap Happy by Sally Schneider
Small Quilts by Marsha McCloskey
Small Talk by Donna Lynn Thomas
Stars and Stepping Stones by Marsha McCloskey
Template-Free™ Quiltmaking by Trudie Hughes
Template-Free™ Quilts and Borders by Trudie Hughes
Threads of Time by Nancy J. Martin
Women and Their Quilts by Nancyann Johanson Twelker

Tools
6" Bias Square®
8" Bias Square®
Metric Bias Square®
BiRangle™
Pineapple Rule
Rotary Mate™
Rotary Rule™

Video
Shortcuts to America's
        Best-Loved Quilts

Many titles are available at your local quilt shop. For more information, send $2 for a color catalog to That Patchwork Place, Inc., PO Box 118, Bothell, WA 98041-0118.